IMAGES OF ENGLAND

HORSHAM STREETS

IMAGES OF ENGLAND

HORSHAM STREETS

SYLVIA BARLOW

TEMPUS

Dedication:

For Julia and Chris, very special people, without whose help and encouragement this book would not have been written.

Sylvia Barlow
2007

My Mum, Sylvia, spent many happy hours (and several frustrating ones !) doing the research for this book.

Although she finished writing it and selecting the photographs, she sadly died before seeing it published.

She wrote it because of her interest in the local history of her adopted town and was not worried whether it made her any money. Because of this, I have decided that any royalties that would have been due to Mum will be donated to the local Girl Guides instead. The Movement was an important part of her life and I feel she would have thought this a good idea.

I am proud of her achievement in writing this book and I hope you enjoy reading it as much as I did.

Julia Farrow
2007

First published 2007

Tempus Publishing Limited
The Mill, Brimscombe Port,
Stroud, Gloucestershire, GL5 2QG

British Library Cataloguing in Publication Data.
A catalogue record for this book is available from the British Library.

ISBN 978 0 7524 4305 8

Typesetting and origination by Tempus Publishing Limited
Printed in Great Britain

Contents

Acknowledgements

Norman Hewell, whose knowledge of twentieth-century streets was the inspiration for, and basis of, this book; Chris Farrow for the excellent contemporary photographs; Horsham Museum Society for their permission to use material from their archives.

My thanks to Elizabeth Vaughan, Maureen Radbourne, Susan Djabri, Jeremy Knight, Curator of Horsham Museum and all the museum staff and all the staff at Horsham Library, for their assistance in making this book possible.

Much of the information for this book was gleaned from the many excellent books on local history in Horsham Library.

Where applicable, every endeavour has been made to contact copyright owners of material used in this book. If anyone has been missed, this was not intended or deliberate.

Introduction

Firstly, a brief overview of how Horsham developed through the ages. Bones and fossils of prehistoric dinosaurs and iguanadons, arrowheads, flint tools and pottery from the Bronze and Iron Ages and evidence of Roman occupation have all been discovered. However, the first written records begin in 947 AD with the charter by which the Saxon King Eadred granted Horsham, part of the manor of Washington, to Eadric. One theory as to how Horsham got its name is that it is a Saxon name meaning horse settlement or horse trading which seems to have taken place here from very early days. Whilst Horsham was not specifically mentioned in the Domesday Book, William the Conqueror did appoint William de Braose as lord of the manor. It was the de Braose family who built the Norman church, St Mary's, and the Rusper Priory and Nunnery in the thirteenth century.

Horsham nestles on the edge of the Weald which was covered with trackways from the south coast from where pigs and cattle were driven up from very early times for summer grazing in what was mainly a wooded area. Traces of Roman occupation have been found and Stane Street, a Roman road, passes quite close to Horsham. There was much heath land but this was poor soil and only good for hunting and so there were many deer parks. Some of the hunting lodges gradually became fortified and were really castles – Bramber, Sedgwick, Steyning, Chennelsbrook and of course Arundel among others. These were initially aimed at reminding the local people that the Normans had conquered England and were subsequently used as a defence against further invasions from France.

Horsham has its own forest, St Leonard's, complete with mythical dragon. This myth was probably embellished by the smugglers, who had their own routes through the forest on the way to London, to deter busybodies from venturing there. Iron working in the forest was a very important industry for many centuries; arrowheads were big business in the fifteenth and sixteenth centuries. The hammer ponds which powered the hammers working the iron are still there today. The forest also provided the wood needed for the charcoal burners, essential to the industry.

Where the soil is suitable, the land has been farmed from Saxon times right through to the twentieth century. Gradually, land owners from near the south coast extended their holdings northwards, built dwellings and people began to meet here. Slowly Horsham began to grow, establishing itself as a market town serving and being served by the surrounding farms and villages. It became well known for its sheep, cattle and corn markets; charters for markets having been granted by the King from the thirteenth century. There were also poultry and local produce markets. Important medieval families built properties succeeded by the rich and influential of later centuries but life continued relatively undisturbed for centuries as Horsham's location was not of any great national strategic importance.

The land was dotted with windmills and water mills – Prewett's Mill in Worthing Road was still producing good quantities of flour into the twentieth century. There were orchards and hop fields with many breweries and, until very recently, King & Barnes Brewery on the Bishopric was still going strong. There were at least three tanneries, one in the Worthing Road, one in Brighton Road and another in Depot Road, as there was no shortage of hides due to the cattle markets. The quarrying of Horsham stone used for roofing and paving was also a thriving industry. The clay soil of the area gave rise to brick making, another important business, and there were several brickyards in the Horsham area.

It was only after the Enclosure Act of 1812 that much of the development began. While the act deprived the poorer people of their right to collect firewood, graze their livestock and garner what they could from the common land, it meant that the land could be bought by the wealthy gentry. The Duke of Norfolk and Robert Hurst became two of the biggest land owners, mainly to the north and east of the town. Indeed, right into the twentieth century, much of the land was owned by the Church and half a dozen rich and powerful families who built large houses and leased out their farms and smaller properties. The look of the landscape began to change as farm boundaries were delineated with hedges and fences and these farms nibbled into the edges of the common, the heath and the forest. The south and west of the town remained largely undeveloped.

The advent of the railways from the middle of the nineteenth century made the transportation of goods much quicker; trade increased and Horsham began to prosper.

More and more shops began to appear alongside the markets catering for all the needs of the local people. 'Le weste streete' has always been a shopping area as has the Carfax, and Middle Street with its butchers' shops. Many shops and trades were often kept in the family for several generations. By the twentieth century, shops we remember, or still have, were appearing such as Boots, Woolworths, International Stores and so on. As horses gave way to cars, garages appeared, while some trades such as blacksmiths and farriers declined. Even so, as late as the nineteenth century, pedestrians had to contend with herds of cattle being driven to market especially along North Street. Because prosperity was rather late in coming to Horsham there had not been that much rebuilding of property which is why so much has been recorded and considerable traces can still be seen today together with many old documents, photographs and artefacts.

Horsham has been returning members to parliament since the late thirteenth century – one of the first towns in the land to do so. Despite the town's many pubs (upwards of fifty at one time!) and rather a reputation for drunkenness, especially at election time, the Temperance Movement was also strong and there were temperance hotels in Market Square and the Carfax. There are still many different religious denominations catered for, covering a wide spectrum of beliefs.

With the increase in literacy and methods of printing there were at least two publishing firms in Horsham and several solicitors' offices by the eighteenth century. Nowadays, there are also over twenty estate agents and many building societies. Clean water was provided by the waterworks from the late nineteenth century when the gasworks were also built. The gasworks were situated where the new YMCA 'Y Centre' building is now. Electricity arrived at the beginning of the twentieth century when the power station was built in Stanley Street.

Horsham has been honoured with several Royal visits. The Prince of Wales (later Edward VII) laid the foundation stone for the new Christ's Hospital School in 1897. In 1967 the Queen Mother laid the foundation stone for St Mary's School and attended a service at St Mary's church when she formally opened the refurbished Memorial chapel. Most recently, in 2003, during HM the Queen's visit to Christ's Hospital for their centenary, Her Majesty formally opened the new Capitol Arts Centre in North Street and unveiled the Horsham Heritage Sun Dial in The Forum. The Sun Dial depicts the history of Horsham and is well worth looking at.

Horsham has always had many thriving clubs and societies and today can boast over 200 representing the interests of young and old alike. The town can also be proud of its bands and live music was, and still is, performed regularly in the bandstands in both the Carfax and the park. Christ's Hospital band also figures strongly in town events. In times past, parades and processions were regular features in the town and until very recently there was still a Horsham carnival and fair in the summer. Charters for fairs have been granted to the town since the thirteenth century; the July fair lasted for several days culminating with entertainment after the serious business of buying and selling. Produce markets are still held weekly in the Carfax and West Street. Horsham festival and funfair is held in the autumn and a ceremony and funfair for the switching on of the Christmas lights takes place in the Carfax and all these events are well supported.

Both adults and children swam in the pond at Mill Bay from early times until the first half of the twentieth century. There was a concrete roller skating rink in the Brighton Road. Just behind St Mary's church is the Garden of Remembrance to the fallen in the First World War. Although now superseded by The Pavilions in the Park opened in 2002, an open air swimming pool, built in Horsham park in 1934, had a very ceremonious opening by no less a personage than Sir Ofori Atta, KBE, King of Akyem Abuakwa, from Africa's Gold Coast (he had local friends!).

Horsham has had military associations for many years. During the early nineteenth century Army regiments were garrisoned here during the Napoleonic Wars. Following the Crimean War later in the nineteenth century, a Volunteer Corps was raised, based at the Drill Hall, and this became the 4th Sussex Regiment during the First World War. Canadian and British troops were stationed here, as were members of the Royal Ordnance Corps during the Second World War. Thankfully, Horsham did not suffer too severely from damage during the Second World War, but there were nearly 300 incidents and many bombs. Local defence units were very active and the war effort well supported. Enough money was raised to buy a Spitfire and, together with Crawley Village, a submarine. Horsham also gave a home to many evacuees.

London can still be reached by train or car and the journey is quicker than it was by foot or coach and horses but some days not by much! Horsham is, of course, within very easy reach of Gatwick Airport. The very modern bus station in Worthing Road was opened in 2003.

Many nationally and locally well-known people are mentioned with the streets either where they lived or which are named after them. Many other streets are named for the farms over which they have been built. Monuments, special buildings and other things of interest are also recorded in the streets where they are situated.

Street names give us glimpses back into the past – they commemorate the people who lived there, their occupations, what was happening in our town in earlier centuries and how national events such as the Battle of Trafalgar and the Napoleonic Wars have influenced the development of the town. The first streets were named North, South, East and West – a very good start! These were the major roads into and out of the town to other parts of the country. Further streets radiated outwards or linked existing streets and gradually the town evolved. It is still thriving, still bustling, still with the feel of an independent market town with a sense of its own identity – still a good place to be living some ten centuries later.

A

Agate Lane (before 1900)

The Agates were an established local family who had been farmers and corn merchants since the sixteenth century. In the late nineteenth century the family owned land in Rusper Road. Alfred Agate owned Parsonage Farm and at one time leased a house in Trafalgar Road. The family also owned a timber yard near the station (see North Street).

Albery Close (1950s)

This is named for William Albery, a saddler, who helped establish Horsham Museum and donated many documents and records of the town together with his magnificent collection of horse bits. He was also a talented musician and was co-founder of the Recreation Silver Band in 1900 (see West Street).

Alder Copse (1950s)

A stand of trees known as Alder Copse is still shown on maps as being part of Denne Park so this road could have been named for this.

Allcard Close (1970s)

The Allcard family owned Wimblehurst house in the early 1900s and the nurseries which were part of the estate were known as Wimblehurst Nurseries. There is also a ward in Horsham Hospital named after the Allcards (see Wimblehurst Road).

Amundsen Road (1970s-1980s)

This is named in honour of Roald Amundsen who was the first person to reach the South Pole in 1911, ahead of Scott's ill-fated expedition.

Arthur Road (late 1800s)

Named after Arthur, Duke of Connaught, who was the seventh child of Queen Victoria, born in 1850.

William Albery's collection of horse bits as they were displayed in Horsham Museum. An exhibition depicting Albery's workshop is now in the museum.

The Recreation Band in 1901 which was co-founded by Willam Albery in 1900.

Ashleigh Road (before 1938)

There used to be a large house here named Ashleigh which was owned at one time by the Lintott family. The name dates back to the fourteenth century when a William de Esshely (later spelt as 'Ashleigh') owned property here. The house was demolished and new houses built in the 1960s.

Athelstan Way (1960s)

Stan Parsons was a locally well-known man in the twentieth century, often referred to as 'Mr Horsham'. He named several streets with Saxon names: this one, Aylwyn, Cedric, Godwyn and White Hart Courts and Hengist Close (see Stan's Way).

B

Bailey Close (1990s)

This is perhaps a reminder that the motte and bailey castle of Chennellsbrook, built in the late thirteenth century, once stood close by. The Normans built this type of castle as they considered it the best method of defence. There was also a moated house nearby, dating from around the same time as the castle which was owned from very early times by the Hurst family and was still in their possession right up to the nineteenth century (see Chennells Way and Hurst Road).

Bakehouse Barn Lane (late 1980s)

This recalls the time when Park Farm covered this area (see Pondtail Road).

Barttelot Road (1893)

Named for Sir Walter Barttelot who was MP for West Sussex from 1887 until his death in 1893. When the police station, built in 1894, was in this road it was the county headquarters and therefore displayed a red rather than a blue lamp. John Haigh, the infamous acid bath murderer, was held in the cells here before appearing before the magistrates in the Town Hall (see Market Square).

Left: Stan Parsons known as 'Mr Horsham' who worked tirelessly on behalf of the town.

Opposite: The Bishopric in 1904.

Belloc Close (1960s and 1970s)

Poet Hilaire Belloc who died in 1953 lived close to Horsham at Shipley. He bought Shipley Mill in 1905 and lived in the house close to the mill which used to be the village shop. It is still a working mill open to the public.

Ben's Acre (1979)

This is named after Ben, a horse belonging to Helen Davis whose parents owned this land. Ben used to graze in these fields.

Bethune Road (1950)

The Bethune family were related by marriage to the Eversfields who owned Denne Park. With no direct heirs the property passed to the Bethune family in 1903 and they changed their surname to Eversfield (see Denne Road).

Bishopric

Originally called the Archbishopric from when the Archbishop of Canterbury owned the land here in the fifteenth century. He was granted a charter to hold a market here, and the Green Dragon Inn which also dates from this time, was possibly used as the administrative centre for the market. Manorial courts were held in the Green Dragon up until the 1700s. Cattle markets continued to be held along the Bishopric right up to the First World War when they were moved to Nightingale Road next to the railway yard.

The Green Dragon pub which was possibly used as an administrative centre for the markets held in the Bishopric from the 1400s and still going strong.

The Kings Arms has long served those attending the markets in the Bishopric and is still popular today.

Henry Burstow, born in the Bishopric in 1826. His recollections were published by William Albery as *Reminiscences of Horsham.*

Still to be seen are a few very old cottages and the King's Arms pub which would have catered to the market crowds from medieval times.

Henry Burstow was born at No. 34 Bishopric in 1826. He became a cobbler by trade but was also well known for his singing and bell-ringing. He had an excellent memory and his recollections were written down by William Albery and published as *Reminiscences of Horsham* in 1911 when Henry was eighty-five. He died at his home in Spencers Road in 1916.

A relative, Edward Burstow, invented the Pentacycle, nicknamed the 'Hen and Chickens' because of its design. This was an adaptation of the pennyfarthing bicycle and had one big wheel with two small wheels on either side. It was trialled briefly by the Post Office but never went into production. A replica can be seen in Horsham Museum.

Fronting onto the Bishopric and running up Springfield Road (where King's Gate flats have just been built) was the King & Barnes Brewery.

Blackbridge Lane

This was originally known as Fatting Barn Lane as cattle were driven along here to Needles Farm to be fattened up for market. Before the housing developments from the 1950s onwards Needles Farm covered much of this area and the farm house Netherledys, near the junction with the Worthing Road, is still lived in today.

Netherledys, the farm house in Blackbridge Lane for Needles Farm, still lived in today.

Although there has been a bridge over the river here for hundreds of years, it is not clear why it is known as the 'black' bridge. Could it have acquired the 'black' in the sixteenth century when Rusper and Holbrook were owned by the Dominican monks who were called the Black Friars because of their black habits? These farms were called Blackfriars and Cripplegate which was the part of London where their priory was situated.

Blackhorse Way (1970s)

This is named after the Black Horse Hotel, demolished in the late 1960s, which stood on the corner of West Street (opposite Wilkinsons). By the 1860s, corn and poultry markets were held in the newly built Corn Exchange next to the hotel. When the exchange closed in the early 1900s, the hotel took over the premises and converted part of them into a ballroom.

This hotel was where the Sussex County Cricket Club members stayed when they played their county matches in Horsham during Cricket Week in June. The Horsham Cricket Club organised the carnival which was held in the town on the Thursday of Cricket Week (see Cricketfield Road).

The Black Horse Hotel which stood on the corner of West Street and Worthing Road until it was demolished in the late 1960s.

Blatchford Road (1970s)

Robert Blatchford was a leading socialist and writer of thirteen books, including *Merrie England* which sold over 2 million copies. In 1891 Blatchford founded the *Clarion* newspaper which was first published in Manchester. He hoped to convert England to socialism but actually upset many by supporting the Boer War and sales of the *Clarion* fell. Sales revived when Blatchford's political views veered to the right causing him to advocate the British Empire. Publication ceased in 1931.

He moved to Horsham in 1914 and lived in Blatchford House until his death at the age of ninety-two in 1943. The house fronted onto Kings Road and part of the garden was used to build Lintott Gardens named after the engineering branch of the Lintott family (see Lintott Gardens).

Blunts Way (1980s)

North Parade was once called Blunts Causeway as Samuel Blunt built Springfield Park House in 1758. The house has now been converted into apartments (see Springfield Road). Blunts Way was built in the grounds of the house.

Bostock Avenue (1930s)

Dr Edward Bostock and his wife, Sarah, lived first in North Street and then in the Causeway. They had eleven children but three sons were killed in the First World War. Born in 1843, Dr Bostock was a surgeon who practised at Horsham Hospital. He was also a governor of Collyer's School, chairman of the board for the Union Workhouse Hospital in the 1890s (in Crawley Road), chairman of Horsham District Council and a JP in the first years of the 1900s. He was a very much respected member of the community.

Bowling Green Lane

This recalls the bowling green which was here in the 1700s.

Boxall Walk (1960s and 1970s)

This is named after Fred Boxall's family. The Fred Boxall who lived in the mid-1800s was a local entrepreneur. He also owned iron and brass foundries.

Bridges Court (1980s)

Mr F.W. Bridges, who was chairman of Horsham Urban District Council in the 1960s, ran a cloth shop in the Carfax (where Panino's now stands).

Opposite: Brighton Road, 1910.

Right: Billy Law, champion town crier in 1912, who lived in Brighton Road.

Brighton Road

From very early days this was, and still is, the route out of Horsham to Brighton. Houses were being built along here by the 1830s and some still exist.

William 'Billy' Law lived in Brighton Road. He was an ostler, looking after the horses at the Kings Head Inn, and a town crier. In 1912, he won the All England Town Criers competition against forty other entrants. His bell can be seen in Horsham Museum.

Mrs Nellie Laughton lived in this road (see Laughton Road).

Up until the mid-twentieth century, the far end of East Street near Bedford Road was known as East Parade but is now part of Brighton Road. The Olympia Skating Rink was built in 1864 and was opposite East Parade School. This school is now the Teacher Professional Centre (see also Tanyard Close and South Grove).

Bryce Close (1970s)

David Bryce ran a furniture store in East Street in the mid-twentieth century. He was also a councillor and involved in many local issues. The David Bryce Day Centre for the elderly is at the end of New Street

Bunting Close (1970s)

This estate was developed by the building firm of Buntings.

The Teacher Professional Centre, formerly East Parade School, in Brighton Road.

Olympia skating rink in Brighton Road, roughly opposite Clarence Road, at the beginning of the twentieth century.

C

Carfax

The precise origins of the word 'Carfax' are lost but two suggestions are either that it derives from *quatre vois* for the four streets originally leading off it or that it comes from *Skar Folkes* meaning that it was 'scarce of people', i.e. an empty area. The Carfax has always been, and still is, the hub of Horsham. Being a large empty space it most likely came to be used as a meeting and trading place for the folk who drove their pigs and cattle up from the south coast to summer pasture on the Weald. It gradually became a market place and a Royal Charter for a market and fair was first granted in the early 1200s. With dwellings in addition to the settlement around East Street and St Mary's being built, the tracks began to be streets and to be named, very sensibly, North, South, East and West as the routes to and from Horsham to the wider world. Subsequently more streets radiated out and linked up the main streets.

At various times the Carfax has been the site of two gaols and a place of public punishment and the area, roughly where the bandstand is located, was also known as Gaol Green. The first gaol, from about the 1500s to 1640s stood on the corner of the Carfax and North Street and although the gaoler's house is still there it cannot really be seen as it has been much altered, re-roofed and re-faced and is inside the shops there. The gaol was behind the house running up North Street. The second gaol, built in 1640, was on the north side of the Carfax. This was used until the late 1700s, falling more and more into disrepair. In 1853 the Michell family bought the building, gutted it and built Grandford House as their family home. It then became the post office before finally being demolished in 1972 and a new office block, still called Grandford House, was built.

Replica stocks and a whipping post are sited near the entrance to Swan Walk – the originals are in Horsham Museum. Bull baiting was a cruel but popular sport up until the mid-1800s when it was banned by law. This took place in the Carfax and the bull ring to which the bull was tethered, together with its metal spike which was driven into the ground, can also be seen in Horsham Museum.

From medieval times coaching inns catered for people and goods travelling to the south coast, London, Guildford, Windsor and Oxford. The Crown built in 1805 and the King's Head dating from the seventeenth century are two which are still there today (King & Chasemore's offices are on the site of the Lamb Inn). There were many other inns and at one time Horsham had the dubious honour of having over fifty pubs and a reputation for drunkenness! Four fairs a year were held here so the pubs would have done good trade. In the late nineteenth century the Inland Revenue office was situated in the King's Head and the sign can still be seen on the wall.

The Carfax in 1890.

A cattle market was held in the Carfax from medieval times up to the mid-1800s when it was moved to the Bishopric. The Crawley & Horsham Hunt met here on Boxing Day from the mid-1800s until the late twentieth century. The Jubilee Fountain was erected in 1897 in honour of Queen Victoria's Diamond Jubilee. It was moved in 1947, lost to view for a while, but has now been re-erected outside the Black Jug pub in North Street. The bandstand was also built in the 1890s. The War Memorial, erected in 1920, was moved to a different position in the 1990s and now commemorates the fallen from both World Wars.

Marks & Spencer and Boots now stand on the site of the Capitol Cinema, later the Capitol Theatre, which was built in 1923. Next door to the cinema in what is now Medwin Walk, was a medieval property called Bornes which was demolished in the 1970s.

It was at the Theatre Royal (near to the Stout House Inn) in 1953 that Sir Michael Caine made his debut as assistant stage manager with walk-on parts, gradually moving on to larger roles.

Caterways (1950s)

This is an old Sussex word used to describe farm fields where, in relation to the farm house, they ran crossways (caterways) rather than longways away from the house.

Grandford House. Today an office block, in the eighteenth century this was the site of the second gaol in the Carfax.

This floorboard with carved initials and the date of 1765 was discovered during building work and had been in the second gaol in the Carfax sited where Grandford House is today, near to the post office.

Causeway

'Causeway' means raised footpath so it is likely this was a wet and muddy track to St Mary's church although until the 1500s it was known as South Street. It is thought that a wooden church stood here in Saxon times but there are no records. The tower and the north-west corner are the only remaining parts of the Norman church, consecrated in 1247. There are some medieval wall paintings on the west wall but these were whitewashed over in the 1953 refurbishment. Much restoration and refurbishment has been undertaken through the centuries, particularly in the 1860s when the church was in danger of collapsing. The present magnificent east window was installed then. Throughout the church there are many windows, monuments and tablets in memory of Horsham folk over the centuries, including an effigy of Sir Thomas de Braose who died in 1395, various members of the Hurst, Lintott, Padwick, Oliver and Bostock families, the Shelley chapel and war memorials. The de Braose family were responsible for building the church and gave the revenues from both the church and the town to the Benedictine Nunnery at Rusper. These revenues were granted in the thirteenth century and continued until the Dissolution in the 1500s.

Many medieval houses, some with Georgian façades, still line the Causeway and several houses, including Flagstones immediately next to the church which dates back to before the 1600s, still have Horsham stone on the roof. Minstrels was originally built in the fifteenth century as two houses but is now just one property. Several of the houses were both homes and workplaces and many tradesmen lived here. An avenue of lime trees were first planted along the road in the late eighteenth century.

The Crown Hotel in the Carfax built in 1805, was once a very busy coaching inn.

Lintott premises in the Carfax where they had a wholesale grocery business from the mid-1800s.

Bandstand in the Carfax where live music is still performed today. The Carfax is not quite so empty as it was in 1890!

In the churchyard next to Flagstones lies buried a lady called Helena Bennet. She was a Muslim who lived in Horsham having been deserted by her husband. She died in 1853 and her grave is aligned to face Mecca.

Since the 1940s Horsham's excellent museum has been housed in another medieval house known as Causeway House (No. 9). This was lived in for a few years by Robert Hurst junior. His sister Sarah Hurst lived there for around ten years until her death around 1800. It is well worth a visit both to see Causeway House itself and for all the records and artefacts stored there.

There is a post just past Horsham Museum on the edge of the road that states during the Second World War there were concrete pyramids on both sides of the Causeway as anti-tank devices in the event of invasion. These were given the name of 'dragon's teeth' but have nothing to do with the legendary dragon in St Leonard's Forest! Some can still be seen in Chesworth Lane.

Another house was owned by Sir Timothy Shelley who was briefly an MP for Horsham in the 1790s and a big landowner in Sussex. He was also the father of Percy Bysshe Shelley, the poet, who was born in Broadbridge Heath (see Shelley Road). In the 1840s this house was leased by the headmaster of Collyer's School, William Pirie.

The Causeway in 1908.

Minstrels, situated halfway along the Causeway, was originally two houses when built in the fifteenth century but is now one property.

Helena Bennet's tomb in St Mary's churchyard where she was buried in 1853 facing Mecca as she was a Muslim.

Horsham Museum housed in a medieval hall house in the Causeway.

Concrete pyramids known as 'dragon's teeth', which were built on either side of the Causeway as anti-tank devices during the Second World War. These can still be seen in Chesworth Lane.

This plaque on the wall of No. 8 Causeway commemorates the women who worked in Horsham Supply Depot housed in this building during the First World War.

The land on the corner of the Causeway and Blackhorse Way was known as the Manor of Hewells and belonged to the Rusper Priory until the Dissolution in 1537. Thereafter it was occupied by various people until 1657 when Cromwell gave the living of Horsham to the Revd Nathaniel Tredcroft, vicar at St Mary's church. By the time he died he was rumoured to be the richest man in Horsham! He built the Manor House around 1700 which, in the twenty-first century, was incorporated in the housing development known as The Manor. Hewells Court was built at the same time. It was the Tredcroft family who leased land behind the church in 1796 to the Government for the army barracks during the Napoleonic Wars. The family were there until the 1850s when it passed to Henry Padwick who acquired it because of unsettled debts.

In the twentieth century the Manor House became the Manor House Preparatory School and subsequently the headquarters of the RSPCA. The present Church Centre is in one of the outbuildings to the Manor House.

George Bax Holmes, the renowned palaeontologist who discovered bones of a giant Iguanadon and the fossilised remains of many other prehistoric creatures, lived at No. 8. He died aged eighty-four in 1887 and left his collection to Brighton Museum (Horsham did not have a museum at that time). He owned much land around Horsham. The Bax Castle pub near Christ's Hospital stands on land where he made some of his discoveries (see also Sandeman Way).

Hammond Innes, the famous author whose family lived at No. 18 in the Causeway was a pupil in the 1920s at the Causeway Preparatory School which was at No. 8, next to Horsham Museum where a plaque in honour of the women who worked in the Horsham Supply Depot during the First World War can be seen on the wall.

Causeway Lodge, No. 10, was part of a medieval building called Hadmans where Dorothea Hurst lived during the 1800s.

Chart Way/Copnall Way (1970s)

These names commemorate Mr Chart, a corn & coal merchant, and Mr Copnall, a photographer. In the twentieth century they ran businesses in North Street in the area now redeveloped by Sun Alliance. When these businesses were flourishing North Street still led directly out of the Carfax.

Chennells Way (1970s)

This is named not only for the stream, Chennells Brook which rises in St Leonard's Forest and runs through to Warnham Ponds, but also for Chennelsbrook Castle. This was the northernmost of a chain of castles built by the de Braose family in the thirteenth century and stood close to Lemmington Way. This was a motte and bailey castle – a motte being a raised mound surrounded by an outer enclosure called a bailey, both of which were surrounded by an outer dry ditch or water moat. As no trace remains it is unlikely the first wooden structure was ever replaced with stone.

Chennelsbrook Farm was built close by in 1296 and is still inhabited today although much altered over the centuries. Located in Rusper Road just near to Lemmington Way, it is probably the oldest building in Horsham.

There was also a moated house in this area.

Chesworth – Lane, Close, Crescent and Gardens (1930s onwards)

'Ceoldred's Worth' or 'Ceoldred's farm' is the Saxon root of the name 'Chesworth' with the farmhouse having been built before 1066. In 1086 the Domesday Book records that it had been granted to William de Braose by William the Conqueror. It remained in the de Braose family for over 300 years except when forfeited to the Crown as the family fell out of favour! By the late 1400s it became the property of the Dukes of Norfolk and stayed in their hands, again except when forfeited to the Crown, for nearly 200 years.

It has been associated with royalty through many reigns. Both Edward I and Edward II stayed here and possibly also King John. In the early sixteenth century it was lived in by Agnes, dowager duchess of Norfolk and grandmother to Ann Boleyn, second wife of Henry VIII and step-grandmother to Catherine Howard. Catherine, who was the fifth wife of Henry VIII, lived at Chesworth from the age of thirteen for around six years during which time she is alleged to have indulged in a couple of affairs. Evidence of these was used against her at the trial which led to her execution in 1542. From around the 1600s, the house has been owned or tenanted by various families including the Eversfields who owned Denne Park.

The house has been demolished and rebuilt several times. The present house, smaller than the grand mansion of earlier times, may probably have been built between the late sixteenth and early seventeenth centuries. Apart from some alterations it varies very little from an inventory of 1780. It sits very graciously in its immaculate gardens and part of the Earl of Surrey's Tower, possibly built around 1520, is still there although reduced in height. Thus there has been a house on this site for 1,000 years or more.

Another use of the name will soon cease as Chesworth School in Kings Road is amalgamating with St Leonard's in 2006 and the new name will be Kingslea.

Churchill Avenue (1970s)

Named for Winston Churchill, Britain's Prime Minister during the Second World War.

Chesworth House as it is today.

Chesworth House today showing the remains of the Earl of Surrey's Tower possibly built *c.* 1520.

Clarence Road (1890s)

Named after the Duke of Clarence, one of Queen Victoria's sons. The famous writer, Hammond Innes, was born here at No. 68 but the family moved to No. 18 in the Causeway towards the end of the First World War.

Collett's Alley

This is named after a Mr Collett who ran the baker's shop here in the early nineteenth century. The shop was actually owned by the Champion family who owned Champion's Mill on the Common (see Kings Road). In the early twentieth century Mr Weston owned this bakery, another in Crawley Road and two windmills.

Collingwood Road/Close (1960s-1970s)

Built in the twentieth century, Hamilton Road and Hardy Close commemorated the Battle of Trafalgar in 1805 by remembering Admiral Collingwood, Lady Hamilton and Captain Hardy (see also Trafalgar Road).

Comptons Lane

Until the late 1800s, Comptons Farm occupied this area. The house called Compton's Brow was built by the Millais family in 1900. J.G. Millais, fourth son of Sir J. Millais the famous painter was a naturalist, author and artist who travelled extensively. In the entrance to Horsham Museum is displayed a very large fish he caught in Canada in 1908. A close friend of J.G. Millais was Frank Wallace who frequently visited him at Horsham and corresponded with him for many years. Frank Wallace was a renowned animal artist and often visited Africa where he met with Cecil Rhodes and helped develop the Kimberley Diamond Mines (see Millais).

J.P. Hornung, a sugar planter, lived at Comptons Lea.

HM the Queen visited Comptons Lane in 1978 when she opened the QEII Silver Jubilee School for children with severe learning difficulties. The school was built over Highlands Farm.

Cook Road (1970s)

Named after the great explorer Captain Cook who voyaged around the world, including Australia, New Zealand and the Pacific islands in the second half of the eighteenth century.

Coolhurst House, home of the Scrase Dickins family, *c.* 1890s.

Coolhurst Lane (late 1970s)

This remembers the Coolhurst Estate in this area from the fifteenth century. By the mid-1800s, the property was inherited by the Scrase Dickins family from the dowager marchioness of Northampton, grandmother to Scrase. The Scrase Dickins family donated generously to St John's church, Coolhurst, built on their property (see Hammerpond Road). In the twentieth century the house was used as St John's College but has now been divided into several houses.

Cootes Avenue (1950s)

This estate was built in the 1950s over Cootes Farm. The farmhouse stood where the Coot pub is now and the Fair View pond was the farm pond. In the eighteenth century the farm was owned by the Shelley family.

Copperfields (1990s)

When the developers bought the Coolhurst Estate it was believed that there was a connection to Charles Dickens although the owners of the estate were surnamed Dickins. It therefore seemed apt to name this road after Charles Dickens' book – *David Copperfield*.

Corunna Drive (1959)

This was where the Army Depot building stood in the early 1800s and is named after the famous battle of Corunna in 1808 during the Peninsular Wars (as a result of Napoleon's invasion of Spain and Portugal). Sir John Moore, who commanded a Rifle Brigade stationed in Horsham, died at Corunna while in command of the English Army, and this road is named for him. It was after this battle that Arthur Wellesley was created Viscount and then a few years later, Duke of Wellington.

Cottingham Avenue (1951)

Alfred Cottingham was a commander of the St John Ambulance Brigade in the mid-twentieth century when the ambulance station was in Park Street.

Crawford Gardens (1970s and 1980s)

Mr Crawford, a headmaster of Horsham Technical School, lived in Kings Road. Crawford Gardens, off Kings Road, was built where he used to live.

The Horsham Technical School used the prefabs in Comptons Lane as classrooms. The prefabs belonged to the Forest Hospital (which had formerly been the Workhouse). Their use ceased when Crawley Technical College was built.

Cricketfield Road (1930s)

As the name implies, down here is the cricket club ground. This area used to be known as Barrack Field. The barracks, adjacent to the field, were built in 1796. In 1800 the Duke of York raised the first Rifle Regiment to be trained as sharpshooters and they were stationed here. After the barracks were demolished, cricket was played on the site and Horsham Cricket Club was formed in 1866. The first County Cricket Festival, later known as Cricket Week, took place early in the 1900s (see Blackhorse Way). Nathaniel Tredcroft had leased the field to the town so that the barracks could be built there and in the 1850s Edward Tredcroft had been a keen cricketer.

D

Dale Close (1960s)

A house called Farhalls used to stand here and was at one time occupied by the Dale family. Farhalls Crescent is also a reminder of the old house.

Denne Road

This was probably an ancient trackway running north – south over Denne Hill and remained the route to the south coast through Denne Park until the eighteenth century. There are two possibilities for the name, the first being that it comes from 'dane' as there is a suggestion that there was a Danish encampment here. Credence is lent to this theory with Picts Hill running along the edge of the property – did the two nations do battle here? The second, and perhaps more likely possibility, is that the name is derived from *denne,* the Saxon word meaning woodland pasture, especially swine pasture, as pigs were herded here to graze. In past centuries this road has also been known as Back Lane and Friday Street.

There has been a property, Denne Park, on this land since the thirteenth century which by the mid-1500s was owned by the Eversfield family who built a new house over the old one in 1606. They also owned Chesworth at this time and used much of the stone and bricks from Chesworth to build Denne Park. Ownership by the family, including the Bethunes who were related, lasted until 1947 when the last family member died and the house was converted to apartments. The family was very influential in the town and several of the Eversfield family were MPs for Horsham. There is a painting in Horsham Museum of Charles and Mary Eversfield who in the first half of the eighteenth century were well known for all the good works they did. When Charles died the property went to his sister Olive and then to her nephew William Markwick with the proviso that he changed his name to Eversfield. William's son died young and his widow married Henry Tredcroft. Through his children, ownership passed to the Bethune family who also changed their name to Eversfield (see Bethune Road).

The grounds were extensive and included a deer park. Part of Denne Hill was maintained as a grassed terrace especially for townsfolk to enjoy a walk or a picnic. Tobogganing down the hill was also popular. A magnificent avenue of lime trees leading to the house was planted in the eighteenth century which, although depleted, can still be seen today from the entrance to the property in Worthing Road.

Denne Park House, home of the Eversfield family, taken before 1914.

The magnificent avenue of lime trees leading to Denne Park House which was first planted in the eighteenth century. Even the hurricane of 1987 did not destroy all of the trees!

Denne Hill, a popular place for the townsfolk to visit, 1908.

The present Drill Hall was built in 1927 (the original was in Park Street). The headquarters of the No. 2 Royal Observer Corps was at the back of the hall during the Second World War. It has always been the venue for dances (especially during the Second World War), amateur dramatic productions, exhibitions and other social events. A ball was held there to celebrate the coronation of George VI in 1937.

In the 1530s, Richard Collyer, a Horsham man and a member of the Mercer's Company in London, left money in his will for a school to be built in Horsham. A site was chosen near St Mary's church and the pupils were required to attend regularly at church services. By the 1840s William Pirie, then headmaster at the school, was instrumental in the building of the second Collyer's School as the old buildings had fallen into disrepair (see Piries Place). When Collyer's School moved to Hurst Road in the 1890s, the Denne Road buildings became a girls' school. After this school was demolished, the Queen Mother laid the foundation stone of the present St Mary's Primary School in 1967 ...a school has therefore stood on this site for over four centuries. Sir Bysshe Shelley, grandfather to the poet, lived in Arun House next door to the school (see also Shelley Road and court).

Three generations of the Hurst family are buried in Denne Road cemetery as are many members of notable Horsham families along with ordinary folk.

The Drill Hall in Denne Road, built in 1927.

Collyer's School when it was in Denne Road before the new school was built in Hurst Road in the 1890s.

Depot Road

This area was all part of the extensive Common and was laid out after the Enclosure Act of 1812. It is so named because there was a large armoury (depot) here during the Napoleonic Wars. The depot was sold in 1827.

Millais Girls School is also situated here, named after the famous artist whose family lived nearby in Comptons Brow (see Comptons Lane).

Dickins Way (1978)

Named after Scrase Dickins whose family estate was here (see Hammerpond Road and Coolhurst Lane).

Doomsday Green and Gardens (before 1830)

Doomsday Green was once a small hamlet. The origin of the name is unknown but it is suggested that the farmer here was called Doomsday and so there is no connection with the Domesday Book. St Leonard's Fair used to be held in this area in November and was chiefly a market for Welsh cattle.

Dutchells Copse (1980s)

A large house and grounds stood here called Dutchells. A Dutchells Copse is shown on old maps in the same area.

E

Earlswood Close (1980s)

Originally there were houses here for the staff of the Forest Hospital which was the former Union Workhouse (Union here means the union of the villages and parishes locally). Forest Hospital was used as the Canadian base hospital during the Second World War. The buildings were later offered to Horsham Hospital for their use but the offer was taken up by Earlswood Hospital (now the East Surrey).

Eastcroft Mews (1980s)

Originally part of the Hills Estate, the land has now been built over. The word 'mews' is most often associated with horses and carriages but its original meaning is 'moult'. Hawks, kestrels, falcons and so on would be housed in a confined space – a mews – during their moulting season.

East Street

Probably where the original settlement began close to St Mary's church, and one of the first named streets. It leads off the Carfax, adjoins Market Square and would have been part of the market. The King's Head pub on the corner of East Street and the Carfax was a thriving coaching inn from the seventeenth century. For a time during the eighteenth century it housed the Inland Revenue office – the sign can still be seen on the wall today.

There are traces of a house called Vigor's Mead (roughly where the hospice shop is today). Vigor was a monk who came from Fecamp Abbey in France in the thirteenth century. At the junction with Denne Road stands another fine medieval house which was called Bishops.

During the Second World War, there was a large air raid shelter in East Street which stretched from Park Street to Barttelot Road.

Beyond the Iron Bridge the street changes its name to Queen Street and then Brighton Road. A few old houses built in the nineteenth century can be seen along this stretch.

Eversfield Road (1930s)

Named after the Eversfield family who owned Denne Park and who were prominent in Horsham and very supportive financially of the fire brigade (see Denne Road).

East Street, *c.* 1870.

The Kings Head hotel on the corner of the Carfax and East Street, *c.* 1900.

Eyles Close (1970s)

Albert Hope Eyles, a local councillor and headmaster of Victory Road Boys School in the 1930s was also a member of the British Legion. Through his connection with the legion he was able to arrange for the British Legion building in North Street to be used as the school's temporary classrooms when part of it burnt down during the Second World War.

F

Fair View (1950s)

This road curves round the pond which was part of Cootes Farm. The view referred to could be the view people would have had of the July fair held in Jews Meadow when it was moved from the Carfax. Jews Meadow stretched from near Springfield Road through to Cootes Farm (see Cootes Avenue).

Falklands Drive

Named after the 1980s Falklands War.

Farhalls Crescent (1960s)

Named after the house which stood where Dale Close has now been built.

Farthings Hill and Walk

These are built on the site of Farthings Farm as is the large roundabout on the A24. There had been a farm here since the fourteenth century which survived until the mid-1940s. It was named for its size, being approximately 40 acres with each of the four sub-tenants holding 10 acres each, i.e. a farthing or quarter (in the same way as a farthing was a quarter of 1d). An old barn dating from the 1500s was still being used as a farm shop until the late 1990s when the site was purchased to build the new Tanbridge School which moved here from its old site in Worthing Road in 1994.

Fishers Court (1980s)

Harry Fisher, born in 1906, was interested in vehicles from an early age. He opened his first garage on this site to repair motorbikes and cars in 1930. By the 1960s he was also dealing in cars. In the 1980s larger premises were required so the business moved to Broadbridge Heath. The family were well known in Horsham. Harry died in Horsham Hospital in 1999 aged ninety-three.

Cobbett's bridge near Fordingbridge Close where a road and a railway cross the river at the same point.

Drain covers still in use today which were manufactured by Lintott Engineering in Foundry Lane from about 1890 until the late twentieth century.

Another example of a Lintott drain cover.

Fitzalan Road (1970s)

This, together with Howard Road, is a reminder that the Duke of Norfolk owned this land.

Fletcher Close (1960s)

The Fletcher family have long been in Horsham. In 1768, Catherine, grand-daughter of Bernard Lintott the publisher from Southwater, married Sir Henry, a director of the East India Co. She was wealthy and it was through her that there are still Fletcher Estates in Southwater to the present day. The Fletchers took a keen interest in Horsham affairs and another Sir Henry was MP in the 1880s.

Fordingbridge Close (1960s)

There has been a crossing over the Arun River since very early days. The old route out of Horsham to Worthing originally ran through Denne Park, crossing the river by Cobbett's bridge at the end of Denne Road (Cobbett was a local landowner in the eighteenth century). This is an unusual site as both a road and a railway cross the river at the same point. In the mid-twentieth century the river was dredged and the banks built up so that this close could be developed.

Forest Road

A very old road running right through St Leonard's Forest (see St Leonard's Forest, Coolhurst Lane, Leechpool Lane and Hammerpond Road).

The Forum (1990s)

A forum is a meeting place and this recently developed, open area (opposite Sainsbury's) is ideally situated having a café at one end and water jets where children can play at the other end. In the middle is the Sun Dial sculpture depicting the history of Horsham which HM the Queen formally unveiled during her visit in 2003. The Forum is large enough to be a good setting for watching various entertainments which are held throughout the year such as the dancing displays given by groups of Morris Men.

Foundry Lane (1890s)

One branch of the Lintott family had an iron foundry here and today their name can be seen on many of the drain covers and manholes in the town. The foundry did not close down until the late twentieth century. Lintott Gardens off Kings Road is also a reminder of this branch of the family (see Lintott Gardens).

G

George Pinion Court (1990s)

Mr Pinion and his wife owned two hairdressing salons in Horsham. Mr Pinion served as a youth court magistrate. He was also twice chairman of the council, an important member of the housing and planning committees and played a key role in the development of the town. He was also a president of the Royal British Legion, with a particular interest in providing homes for ex-service personnel. He died in 2004.

Giblets Lane

Although there were poultry farms in Horsham, the name is not connected but derives from the family who owned land here centuries ago – the Gyblettes.

Gillett Court (1980s)

Mr Gillett was the farmer at South Holmes Farm.

Gilligan Close (1980s)

Named after Arthur Gilligan, the cricketer who played for Sussex from 1920-32 and was their captain from 1922-29. He also captained England in test matches against Australia. In Gilligan Close four blocks of flats are named after Sussex cricketers.

Gladstone Road (1890s)

William Gladstone served several terms of office as British Prime Minister between 1868-96. The street was developed in the 1890s when much building was carried out in Hurst Road which had been laid out between North Parade and the station in the 1860s.

Gordon Road (1890s)

Because of the date when this road was built, it was most likely named for Gen. Charles Gordon who was killed in 1885 defending Khartoum against the Mahdi's troops two days before a relief force arrived.

A stone from Penny bridge which used to cross the Penny stream in Guildford Road just by Blackbridge Lane. The stream now goes underground.

A less likely possibility is that it is named after Lord William Gordon, second son of the third Duke of Gordon, a long established Scottish family. He was a womaniser and a gambler. He met Lady Irwin (see Hills) whilst gambling in London and married her daughter, Frances, in 1781. He was MP for Horsham from 1792-96.

Hearsay tells us that Emperor Haile Selassie of Ethiopia who was overthrown in 1974 and came to England, fell off his bicycle in Gordon Road!

Gorings Mead (1930s)

Sir Harry Goring was a local MP in the early 1700s. The family are still prominent in Sussex.

Greenfields Close, Road and Way (approximately 1970s)

These roads were built over Greenfields Farm owned by the Greenfield family whose property adjoined Lambs Farm.

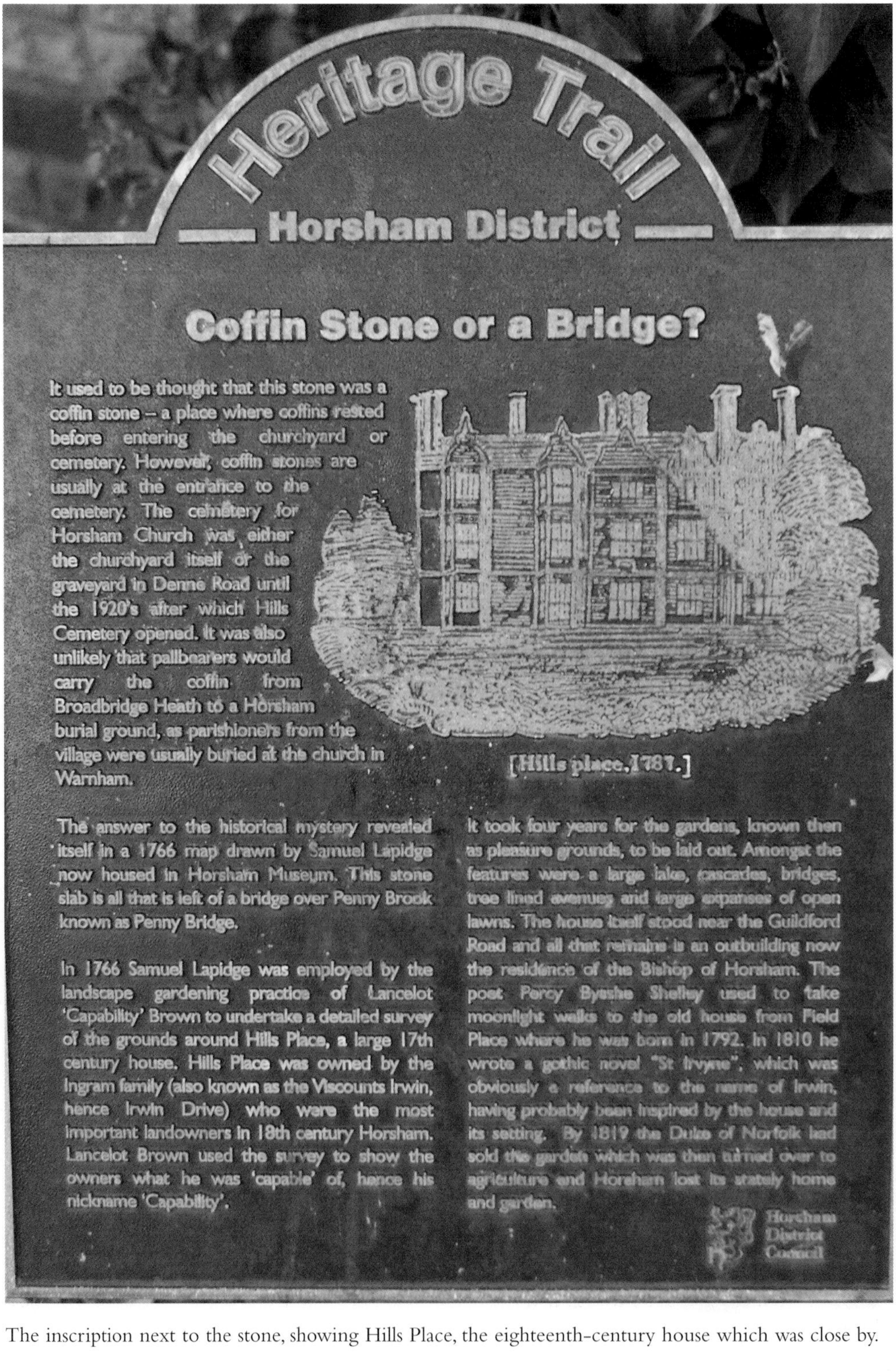

Heritage Trail

Horsham District

Coffin Stone or a Bridge?

It used to be thought that this stone was a coffin stone – a place where coffins rested before entering the churchyard or cemetery. However, coffin stones are usually at the entrance to the cemetery. The cemetery for Horsham Church was either the churchyard itself or the graveyard in Denne Road until the 1920's after which Hills Cemetery opened. It was also unlikely that pallbearers would carry the coffin from Broadbridge Heath to a Horsham burial ground, as parishioners from the village were usually buried at the church in Warnham.

[Hills place, 1787.]

The answer to the historical mystery revealed itself in a 1766 map drawn by Samuel Lapidge now housed in Horsham Museum. This stone slab is all that is left of a bridge over Penny Brook known as Penny Bridge.

In 1766 Samuel Lapidge was employed by the landscape gardening practice of Lancelot 'Capability' Brown to undertake a detailed survey of the grounds around Hills Place, a large 17th century house. Hills Place was owned by the Ingram family (also known as the Viscounts Irwin, hence Irwin Drive) who were the most important landowners in 18th century Horsham. Lancelot Brown used the survey to show the owners what he was 'capable' of, hence his nickname 'Capability'.

It took four years for the gardens, known then as pleasure grounds, to be laid out. Amongst the features were a large lake, cascades, bridges, tree lined avenues and large expanses of open lawns. The house itself stood near the Guildford Road and all that remains is an outbuilding now the residence of the Bishop of Horsham. The poet Percy Bysshe Shelley used to take moonlight walks to the old house from Field Place where he was born in 1792. In 1810 he wrote a gothic novel "St Irvyne", which was obviously a reference to the name of Irwin, having probably been inspired by the house and its setting. By 1819 the Duke of Norfolk had sold the garden which was then turned over to agriculture and Horsham lost its stately home and garden.

Horsham District Council

The inscription next to the stone, showing Hills Place, the eighteenth-century house which was close by.

The Bishop's House, home of the Bishop of Horsham. The previous old building, perhaps either a barn or stabling on the Hills estate, was converted into a house in the 1920s.

Guildford Road

This is an old route out of Horsham from the Bishopric and was once known as the Oxford Road. Just after Blackbridge Lane is a large slab of stone. For a long time it was thought to be a coffin stone, where those carrying a coffin to the churchyard for burial would have rested the coffin for a few minutes. It is, however, an unlikely place for such a stone as it is nowhere near the parish church. It is now known that the stone was part of the bridge over Penny Brook which runs under the road just here. The bridge is clearly shown on a 1766 map which was drawn to assist Capability Brown in designing the grounds for Hills.

Just past the pedestrian lights is Hills Place; the flats called Hills Manor are built on land which was part of a property called Hills. The eighteenth-century Jacobean stately home stood further back from the road and to the west of the flats.

Also in Hills Place can be found the Bishop's House (Hills Barn), now the residence of the Bishop of Horsham. This was either ancient stabling for Hills or demolition material from Hills which was used to build the barn. It was converted to a house in the 1920s (see Hills).

H

Hadmans Close (1970s)

Built in the grounds of Hadmans which was a medieval property at Nos 10-12 in the Causeway. Its land stretched back into Denne Road.

Hammerpond Road

A very old road and so named for the hammer ponds necessary for the iron works in St Leonard's Forest. The iron ore was readily available and so too was the timber to produce the charcoal necessary to power the hammers. Iron working was a very important industry for Horsham for many centuries.

The Forest church – St John's, Coolhurst – was built in 1838 on the estate belonging to the Dickins family. Some of the money for this was raised from horse races which used to be held in the Forest and Scrase Dickins also made a generous contribution (see Coolhurst Lane and Dickins Way). This church was also known as the Doomsday church; partly because it was near the hamlet of Doomsday Green but also because the forest was said to be haunted, especially this stretch of road.

There were always many beech and oak trees in the forest. Both trees were important as beech nuts and acorns were a main source of food, known as pannage or mast, for pigs. Around 200 yards up the road from the church is a very old and magnificent tree known as the sun oak, standing at the entrance to Sun Oak Farm. This was one of the entrances to St Leonard's Park, a large estate near to Hampers Lane. A sun oak plantation is still shown on current maps.

There was a POW camp near to the church during the Second World War.

Harwood Road (1980s)

This was built as a bypass for Roffey and there was once a large house called Harwood roughly on the corner of Kings Road and Harwood Road. It was owned by the Lyons family who were distantly related to the Queen Mother. Bowes Close with the same connection is built on the former estate land.

The hammerpond, one of several ponds in St Leonard's Forest, used in the iron-working industry which flourished in the forest over many centuries.

Hammerpond house, possibly once the home of an ironmaster working in the forest.

The magnificent sun oak tree which stands at the entrance to Sun Oak Farm in Hammerpond Road.

Hawksbourne Road

This land once belonged to the ancient manor of Hawksbourne. Hawksbourne Farm, dating from the seventeenth century, is still lived in today and is on the road to Rusper.

Haybarn Drive (1990s)

A reminder that this is built over Park Farm (see Pondtail Road).

Heath Way (1970s)

This area once formed part of the ancient North Heath and is also neatly named after Edward Heath, a British Prime Minister.

Hengist Close (1980s)

At one time it was thought that the Saxons, Horsa and Hengist, might have been involved in the beginnings of Horsham but this has been disproved (see Stan's Way).

Hills Place showing the remains of the Elizabethan farmhouse which once stood on this site.

Hernbrook Drive (late 1930s)

The house called Hernbrook, now demolished, was at one time lived in by the Whitehouse family. Members of the family were directors of the brick works at Warnham and Southwater in the early twentieth century (see Sandeman Way).

Highlands Road

This used to be known as Grubb Street and was where, before the nineteenth century, all the town rubbish was dumped. It possibly got its name from the poor folk who would have 'grubbed around' for anything they could use. This was one of the first areas of the Common to be developed after the Enclosure Act of 1812.

Hills Place, Lane and Farm (1980s)

The large imposing mansion called Hills stood back from Guildford Road behind and to the west of where the flats called Hills Manor are now (see Guildford Road). There has been a dwelling on this site since earliest times; Roman remains were found during excavations in the 1980s. A family called Hill lived there in the fourteenth century. The Middletons, another family who owned it, built a new house adjacent to the old Elizabethan farmhouse.

By the late 1600s it was owned by the Ingram family (Viscount Irwin). The Ingram's main residence was Temple Newsom near Leeds but they visited Hills at least once a year and, after the death of her husband in 1702, Lady Isabel Ingram continued to be very prominent politically in opposition to the Duke of Norfolk and the Eversfield family. Lady Irwin presented Horsham with a fire engine (more of a water cart!) in 1780 which was kept at the Town Hall. Capability Brown started work on the grounds in 1786 but no obvious trace can be seen today although some of the trees along Hills Farm Road are very old and could perhaps have been part of his planting (see Guildford Road).

The property was sold to the Duke of Norfolk in 1811. The house was pulled down and rebuilt in 1818. All the properties on the estate were finally demolished in the twentieth century but we still have several reminders in Hills Cemetery, Hills Farm Lane, Ingram Close, Irwin Drive and Middleton Road.

Honeywood Road (1960s)

Named after Mr Honywood (there was no 'e' in his name) who was captain of the Volunteer Fire Service for over twenty years in the late 1800s. He was also a photographer, an artist and an archaeologist. When he was building a new house in West Street a collection of medieval pots and jugs known as the Horsham Hoard was discovered. The hoard can be seen in Horsham Museum along with his portrait.

A general view of Horsham Park

Hurst Road

Named for the Hurst family who have been prominent in the town since the Middle Ages. Several members of the family were MPs for Horsham. In the 1860s the family gave land to the town so that this road could be built down the side of the park to provide a route from North Parade to the station.

In the 1990s the family gave more land so that a new school for Collyer's, the hospital and the first School of Arts & Crafts could be built. The latter was demolished in the early twenty-first century and has been replaced with flats. In the twentieth century, the police station, fire station, law courts and post office depot were also built in Hurst Road.

Robert Hurst was one of the biggest landowners in Horsham. He acquired much of his land from the Duke of Norfolk after they had worked together to get the Common enclosed under the Enclosure Act of 1812 (see North Street). Mention is made in nineteenth-century records of a moated house built near Chennelsbrook Castle in the thirteenth or fourteenth century belonging to the family. They also owned Rusper Nunnery in the nineteenth century and when a new house was being built several skeletons, thought to be those of nuns, were discovered. In one of the graves there was a beautiful twelfth-century chalice and several other religious objects. The chalice is in the British Museum (at that time Horsham did not have a museum).

I

Innes Road (1960s)

Named after Lt-Col. J. Innes who bought Roffey Park around 1880. He was the commanding officer at Roffey Camp at the start of the First World War when the site was used by the 22nd Battalion of the Royal Fusiliers as a training camp for Kitchener's new armies. He has no connection with Hammond Innes, the author who also lived in Horsham (see Clarence Road and Causeway).

Irwin Drive and Ingram Close (1980s)

See under Hills.

J

Jockey Mead (1950s)

Originally part of Needles Farm (see Blackbridge Lane).

Hurst Road about 1890 before development began.

The original entrance to the hospital in Hurst Road built in the 1890s.

Collyer's Sixth Form College, previously the school, in Hurst Road, built in the 1890s when the school moved from Denne Road.

New buildings for Collyer's Sixth Form College in Hurst Road built in 2003.

The Pavilions in Horsham Park, opened in 2003.

K

Kempshott Road (1870s)

Kempshott Road, together with Swindon and Purton Roads, was named by the housing developers who came from the area near Basingstoke. Purton and Swindon are places near to Basingstoke and Kempshott is now part of Basingstoke.

Kennedy Road (1960s)

Named after John F. Kennedy, former President of the USA.

Kentwyns Drive (1930s)

This was the name of the house which stood here. The Macleod family of the Clan Macleod from the Isle of Skye used their house when they came to England. He was the first chairman of Horsham Urban District Council in the 1890s when it took over from the union of local parishes and churches (see also Macleod Road).

Kerves Lane (late 1800s)

Takes its name from Kerves Brook which runs close by. When the gaol was situated in Queen Street executions used to take place at the point where Kerves Lane led off the Brighton Road. There were riding stables here in the mid-twentieth century.

Kidmans Close (1960s)

Named after the Kidmans Arms pub which stood to the right of the present entrance to the Close in Rusper Road.

Kings Road

The road was laid out after the Enclosure Act of 1812 and most likely named for George IV. People would stand along here to watch the condemned on their way to the gallows near Champions Mill. The mill was not far from the corner with Foundry Lane but a little further up Kings Road. The mill blew down in 1860 and the miller was killed but his cottage can still be seen by going down the driveway between Nos 21 and 21a. Ann Cruttendon was possibly the last person to be burnt at the stake here in 1776.

L

Lakeside (1950s and 1960s)

Named because it backs on to Warnham Mill pond.

Lambs Farm Road (1950s and 1960s)

The housing estate was built on the site of Lambs Farm. The farmhouse is still inhabited and stands just into Lambs Farm Road from the Rusper Road end.

Laughton Road (1960s)

Mr Laughton was killed during the First World War and his widow, Nellie, built the Garden of Remembrance (behind St Mary's church) in his memory for all those who died in the First World War. After her husband's death, Mrs Laughton, who lived in Brighton Road, devoted all her time to helping local people. She was a JP, a councillor, worked with the NSPCC and the RSPCA, presented Horsham with its first motorised ambulance and in so many ways was a benefactor of Horsham. She died in 1953 aged eighty-six. The name commemorates them both.

Leechpool Lane (by 1900)

This was once part of St Leonard's Forest where it is reputed that leeches were caught and sold to doctors for bloodletting, a widely used treatment to 'ease the humours of the blood'.

Leggyfield Court (1980s)

This area used to be fields running down to the river and there is a suggestion that the name could derive from 'lag', an old word meaning copse/wood. There was a stand of hazel trees/ coppice so 'lag' could have gone to 'laggy' and thence 'leggy' field.

Leith View Road (1960s)

Before the trees grew too tall, it was possible to see Leith Hill Tower near Dorking some twenty miles away.

Horsham Urban Council Notes

CAPITOL ADVERT FIRM BACKS OUT

MAGNET Advertising Company, who have had exclusive right of advertising on the Capitol safety curtain for a year, have told Horsham Urban Council that they will renew the agreement for another year if the council would reduce the rent from £100 to £50 a year.

The Entertainments and Publicity Committee would not reduce the rent and the company had not said they wished to exercise its option so the agreement has lapsed. Now the committee is to ask present advertisers whether they wish to continue their advertisement on terms to be agreed with the council.

This was reported at Wednesday's council meeting.

* * *

The Housing Committee has refused a request from the developers of Lambs Farm Estate for the exchange of a piece of land on the Lambs Farm Estate for a piece of land of similar size on the council's Littlehaven estate.

* * *

The clerk has told the Building and Town Planning Committee that West Sussex County Council were proceeding with the preparation of plans for the comprehensive re-development of the area around the gas works site.

* * *

The Finance and General Purposes Committee have felt that there are insufficient grounds for raising an objection to the application by Southdown Motor Services Ltd. to the traffic commissioners for fare increases. The company has said that they wish to increase revenue to meet part of the additional cost caused by the further wage award in October.

* * *

for the Prevention of Accidents from £2 2s. to £4 4s. The society has said that no change had been made in the existing rates since 1928.

* * *

Lambs Farm-road and Farhalls-crescent are to be the names of two new roads on the Lambs Farm estate.

* * *

The council agreed that Mrs. M. Berkley-Barton should be appointed head of the welfare section of the Horsham sub-division of the Civil Defence Corps.

* * *

It will cost £250, out of the current district road estimates, to kerb the length of Spencers-road between the cul-de-sac and Percy-road, and to provide a six-foot footpath.

* * *

The council is to insist that a London-road firm should pay the outstanding balance of £10 2s. on a bill submitted by the council for constructing a pavement crossing to their premises.

The firm had stated that the charge was grossly excessive and would only have cost £24 18s. if it had been constructed by contractor. They forwarded a cheque for that amount.

* * *

The Festival Committee is to be granted free use of the Capitol between July 11 and 18 next year, when the Horsham Festival is being held, and on July 10, when Horsham Music Circle are to organise a concert.

50 people. It is expected that the factory will be completed by next autumn.

They are anxious to transfer eight key personnel to Horsham, and it would be necessary to find accommodation for at least six to eight families in Horsham.

* * *

The council approved the surveyor's policy to install smokeless fuel burning grates whenever a replacement was needed in a council house.

* * *

The attention of a council house tenant whose chimney was found to contain a great deal of soot after a chimney fire is to be drawn to his obligation under the conditions of tenancy to keep the chimney swept.

* * *

The Building Plans sub-committee has approved plans for a public house with tenant's flat over and car parking facilities at the junction of Merryfield-drive and Cootes Avenue.

* * *

The Finance Committee rejected a request from the 2nd Horsham Scout Group for a remission of rates in respect of their premises in Swindon-road, in view of the group's financial liabilities due to road charges. The committee felt it was not the responsibility of the council to render assistance in the matter.

Newspaper cutting from the *West Sussex County Times* dated 19 December 1958, reporting on the Council's approval for the names of two new streets – Lambs Farm Road and Farhalls Crescent.

Lintott Gardens (1970s)

There were three well-known branches of the Lintott family. One was the Southwater branch where Barnaby Bernard Lintott, born in 1675, dropped the name 'Barnaby' together with the second 't' from his surname. As Bernard Lintot, he became famous as the publisher of Alexander Pope's translation of Homer's *The Iliad* in 1715. His premises were in Fleet Street in London. A copy of Pope's book can be seen in Horsham Museum.

Another branch of the family started Lintott Engineering in the 1890s at their premises in Foundry Lane. Lintott Gardens are named for this branch of the family. The third branch ran a retail grocery and provisions business originally in South Street. By the mid-1800s the business became wholesale and the family had moved to a large property in the Carfax.

A later Bernard Lintott was three times chairman of the HUDC during the 1920s and 1930s.

Livingstone Road

Built in the mid-twentieth century it incorporated part of Stanley Street, the remainder of which is now Stanley Walk. They were named in honour of Stanley and Livingstone, the famous explorers of the nineteenth century. Victoria Street commemorates the discovery of the famous Victoria Falls in Africa (see Stanley Walk).

London Road

One of the very early routes from the Carfax, it led into Springfield Road and then onto Dorking and London. The start of this road leading out of the Carfax is now pedestrianised (see Medwin Walk). The British School was situated in London Road from around 1827.

At one time there was an animal pound and a house of correction as well as many small tradesmen's and craftsmen's cottages. In the nineteenth century, William Albery owned Ockendons named after a medieval property which had originally stood on the site (see Albery Close and West Street). The Wesleyan chapel, now the Methodist church, was erected in the nineteenth century. There is still an impressive terrace of Regency houses called Sussex Place.

Bernard Lintott in about 1920 who was chairman of the HUDC during the 1920s and 1930s.

London Road in 1911 just showing the blacksmith's premises – still an important trade at that time.

M

Macleod Road (1950s)

Named after the Macleod family (see Kentwyns Drive).

Manor Road (1960 and 1970s)

Possibly named thus because the area was in the old Manor of Hawkesbourne.

Market Square

A very old square, part of the Carfax Market from the fourteenth century. There was a hall where market administration took place. It was built on arches under which market stalls would have been erected. The original market hall was superseded by others and in 1812 the Duke of Norfolk rebuilt it as a town hall with court rooms. The Duke was a keen antiquarian and designed the building to resemble a castle. The three coats of arms depicted on the front wall are the Royal Arms, those of the Duke of Norfolk and those of the town. In 1888, the Town Hall was rebuilt yet again, with the front façade and the cells beneath the building being retained and this is how we see it today.

The arches were boarded up when the assize court sat here from 1300 until 1830 when it was moved to Lewes after the judges complained about the poor state of the building. A magistrate's court was still held here until the mid-twentieth century. In 1949 John Haigh, the infamous acid bath murderer, was brought here, before standing trial in Lewes Crown Court. He was found guilty of killing six people and disposing of their bodies in sulphuric acid.

Elections were held at the Town Hall and it was the scene of many riotous occasions. At the election of 1847, notorious for bribery and corruption, tempers ran high when opposing candidates plied the public with free liquor in an attempt to win their votes. After the election, when there would have been much rejoicing by some and bitterness by others, more trouble ensued, again fuelled by drink.

The building was also the venue for council meetings in the nineteenth century.

The Bear Inn to the right of the Town Hall was sold as a house in 1652. Along with other pubs it served the crowds attending the markets and the elections.

Where Bar Vin is today was once the Anchor Hotel. An inn has stood on this site since the seventeenth century. It was rebuilt in 1900 and the name can still be seen above the entrance. On the same side of the road and a little nearer to the Town Hall was the Temperance Hotel owned and run by Jury Cramp, prominent in the Temperance Movement. He also owned a jeweller's shop (see West Street).

The Town Hall in Market Square with the façade showing the Royal Arms, the arms of the Duke of Norfolk and those of the town, which was retained when the Town Hall was last rebuilt in 1888.

The Bear Inn in Market Square, originally a private house before becoming an inn around 1700.

The Anchor hotel in Market Square, rebuilt in 1900. An inn has stood on this site since the seventeenth century.

Martlets Close (1960s)

Martlet is the Sussex name for a swallow or martin. The martlet is depicted on the county coat of arms but is shown without feet – these are said to be sunk down into Sussex mud!

Medwin Walk

Originally the beginning of the London Road out of the Carfax. It is named after Thomas Medwin who at one time was steward to the Duke of Norfolk and agent for Sir Henry Fletcher. Thomas and his younger son Pilfold were lawyers in the seventeenth and eighteenth centuries, and Pilford especially did a lot of good for the poor people of the town. There were still Medwin lawyers in business here until the middle of the twentieth century.

Near where Boots now stands was a medieval property called Bornes which was demolished in the 1970s (see Carfax). Opposite Boots where King & Chasemore have been in business for over 100 years once stood the Lamb Inn.

Merryfield Drive (1950s)

This road could be aptly named from when folk came here to enjoy the July fair. This had been held in the Carfax since the thirteenth century but was moved to here in 1887 and survived as a funfair until the 1930s.

Some of the fields here were known as Jew's Meadow; the name might come from the Jewer or Juer family who are mentioned in early seventeenth-century records.

At one time this area had been farmland with Cootes Farm, Spencer's Farm and Jew's & Rusham's Farm, the latter only being fields and barns whilst Cootes and Spencer's also had farmhouses.

Cattle were driven to Jew's Meadow to await the markets in the Bishopric and in 1904 the famous Buffalo Bill's Wild West Show was held here for just one day.

Michell Close (1980s)

The Michells were an important family in Horsham from the eighteenth century. They lived at Stammerham which is where Christ's Hospital now stands (see Worthing Road). The family was connected by marriage with the Shelley, Ingram and Middleton families.

Middle Street, originally known as Butchers Row, *c.* 1904.

Middle Street

A very short street which links West and East Streets. Originally known as Butchers Row, it was handily placed for meat coming from the cattle markets in the Carfax. After bull baiting in the Carfax, the carcasses would also have been brought here. Miss E. Gatford owned a property here (see North Street).

Middleton Road (1980s)

This remembers the Middleton family who had owned Hills (see Hills). John Middleton had been an MP in the 1600s.

Millais (1960s)

Named after the Millais family. Sir Henry Millais, the famous painter, or his son John lived nearby in Comptons Brow. There is also the Millais Girls' School.

Moons Lane (1980s)

Thomas Moon was a tanner and leather merchant working here in the 1870s. He also owned the tannery in the Brighton Road.

Morth Gardens

Probably a medieval alley or twittern connecting Denne Road to the Causeway. John Morth built three cottages here for his daughters in the early 1800s. John lived in Springfield Road and was a carpenter. He was a member of the Society of Independents who bought from the Duke of Norfolk a piece of land in Swan Meadow which was behind the Swan Inn (see West Street) on which they built a chapel in 1814. The society became known firstly as the Congregational Church and then the United Reformed Church (see Springfield Road).

Sir George Paich (1867-1957), a financial journalist and economist, was born in Morth Gardens.

Morth Gardens where John Morth built three cottages for his daughters in the early 1800s.

N

Naldrett Close (1970s)

Mr Naldrett lived in Wimblehurst Road in the early twentieth century before moving to Rusper Road. He was secretary of Horsham Charities which, among other things, provided coal for poor and elderly people. As late as the 1960s, Mr Naldrett could be seen in his 'round dress' or Sussex smock when he went walking with the Sussex Wealdsmen.

Needles Close (1980s)

This is built over part of Needles Farm and the farmhouse, close by, is still lived in today (see Blackbridge Lane).

Nelson Road (1870s)

See Trafalgar Road

New Street

From the early 1700s this was known as Pest House Lane when a pest house was built here to house those suffering from infectious or contagious diseases.

When the area was developed after the enclosure of Horsham Common in 1812, it became known as New Street – who would have wanted the old name?

Nightingale Road (before 1900)

Nightingale was the name of the family who farmed Lambsbottom Farm and the farmhouse can still be seen near the North Street end of Hurst Road. It is possible that Lambs Farm and Lambs Bottom Farm had the same owner i.e. the latter was the 'bottom' farm to distinguish it from the former. There are also some other very old buildings at the corner of North Street and Hurst Road.

Norfolk Road and Terrace (by 1900)

These are named for the Dukes of Norfolk who have so many connections with Horsham. The Duke of Norfolk is the Earl Marshall of England and is responsible for organising all royal ceremonies.

Normandy

In the early 1200s, a member of the de Braose family brought with him a brotherhood of monks from Fecamp Abbey in Normandy, France, possibly to assist the nuns at the Priory in Rusper. The brotherhood also ran the almshouses which have been here since the thirteenth century and which were last rebuilt in the twentieth century. There is a connection with a house called North Chapel, close to the station, which was owned by the Norman brotherhood as well (see North Street).

The priest's house stood between the almshouses and the church but was demolished in the nineteenth century. It is believed that there was a well in the Normandy, the water from which was used for christenings in St Mary's church.

There was possibly a bell foundry here in the early seventeenth century – some of the bells were still in use in the nineteenth century.

The Normandy, *c.* 1920.

The magnificent East Window in St Mary's church installed in the 1860s, viewed from the Normandy.

North Heath Lane

This lane ran across the Heath and when the housing estate was built in the 1960s and 1970s the streets were named after different heath plants, e.g. Erica Way, Broome Close, Gorse End. This estate was built over Dendys Farm and the farmhouse dating back to 1630 in the middle of the estate is still lived in. After the demolition of St Mark's church in North Street, a new one was built in North Heath Lane.

Northlands Road

See Ryders Way.

North Parade

Formerly called Blunt's Causeway after Samuel Blunt who built and lived in Springfield Park in the 1700s (see Springfield Road). After the Enclosure Act of 1812 housing was developed to the north of Springfield Park along North Parade which leads on from Springfield Road and joins up with the London Road which led out of the Carfax and heads for Dorking and London.

The flats named Lynwood Court reflect that Lynwood House was one of the first dwellings to be built on the Common after the Enclosure Act of 1812. Lynwood House was occupied in the late nineteenth century by General Keatinge (Rtd) who won a VC in India.

North Street

This was one of the original roads out of the Carfax and led towards Rusper where there was a nunnery which for many years received revenue from St Mary's church and the town. In earlier times the street was called Comewell Street as there was a public well, now buried beneath the council offices. The rural district council offices were in Comewell House before the local councils were amalgamated in 1974.

A very old property dating back to the 1500s called Cockmans stood in North Street. Several prominent families either owned or lived here including the Ingrams, the Michells and the Lintotts. Park House, as it came to be called, was rebuilt in 1770 for John Wicker and then bought by Robert Hurst in 1799. In 1928, the Hurst family sold it to the town and it is now council offices. There was a formal garden beyond which the grounds were farmed by the Hurst family with the pond being part of the farm. The grounds are now Horsham Park with the Pavilions Leisure Centre, a Millennium Maze and other leisure facilities. During the Second World War the park was part of the defences against invasion (see also Hurst Road for more about the family).

North Parade showing the entrance to Springfield Park House, *c.*1900.

North Street before sheep gave way to cars as the main hazard for the traveller, *c.* 1900.

Until the new fire station was built in Hurst Road in the mid-twentieth century it had been next to Park House. Horsham Museum was in Park House during the 1930s before moving to the Causeway in 1941. During excavation work in the 1980s a large medieval well in the cellar was discovered.

The Jubilee Fountain was moved from the Carfax and later repositioned in 1993 in front of the Black Jug (or Jack) pub which was originally the Hurst Arms.

Sun Alliance moved into Horsham in the 1960s and one of their buildings occupies the site where St Mark's church once stood. When the church was built in 1840 remains of an iguanadon were found. Following demolition in 1989 only the spire remains (see North Heath Lane). The construction of Albion Way cut North Street off from the Carfax and the construction of Copnall Way and Chart Way became the pedestrianised route out of the Carfax and into North Street.

The first railway station was built in 1848 and the cattle and poultry markets moved to a site adjacent to the station yard after the First World War. The station (now a listed building) was rebuilt in 1938 when the line was electrified. Hampers and Fillerys farms were once here and one old farm building can still be seen behind the station. Where the Horsham Gates office block now stands was once known as Agate's Corner as the family owned the timber yard here (see Agate Lane).

The back of Park House in the 1860s.

The back of Park House with the scented garden where the picnic was taking place in the 1860s photograph above.

The Jubilee Fountain, originally in the Carfax but repositioned here in North Street in 1993. The Black Jug, formerly the Hurst Arms, can be seen in the background.

The station in 1898.

The old houses which are on the corner of North Street and Hurst Road, dating back several hundred years.

North Chapel in North Street, *c.* 1900.

North Chapel, possibly more than 500 years old, now used as offices.

The Capitol, Horsham's Arts Centre, in North Street.

Near the station there are some very old cottages on the park side of the road and opposite them is a very old house called North Chapel (see Normandy). Miss Elizabeth Gatford owned this house and other property in Middle Street. When she died in 1799, she ensured that she would stay put after death by requesting to be buried in four coffins, one inside the other, but not until she had been dead for a month!

The new Capitol Arts Centre, opened by HM the Queen in 2003, is a conversion of the Ritz Cinema and near here there was a medieval property called Perry Place. This was moved to Mannings Heath and rebuilt as the Golf clubhouse.

Dr Geoffrey Sparrow, born in 1887, lived in several places in and around Horsham. In 1934 the site of his house at No. 5 North Street became the ABC Cinema (roughly where the Horsham Volunteer Bureau is today). In addition to being a doctor doing his rounds on horseback, Dr Sparrow was a keen huntsman and artist. Horsham Museum has a large collection of his paintings and drawings.

O

Old Millmeads (1960s)

There was an old house here called Millmeades built on the meads i.e. the meadows, by Warnham Mill. The 'old' was added in the twentieth century to avoid postal confusion with Hillmead.

Oliver Road (1060s onwards)

Named after Thomas Oliver, the successful Victorian railway engineer who built Tanbridge House (see Worthing Road).

Owlbeech Court, Place and Way

These roads are very close to St Leonard's Forest. This part of the forest, known as Owlbeech Woods, is still a favourite spot with walkers.

P

Padwick Road (1970s)

Mr Padwick, lawyer, moneylender and a gambler was involved in many enterprises, more for his own benefit than that of the town. He owned the Manor House in the Causeway from the middle of the nineteenth century having acquired it from the Tredcroft family in settlement of debts (see Causeway). One of Mr Padwick's sons, a doctor, lived in North Street where a Sun Alliance building now stands and the other son, a keen photographer, lived in the large Victorian house Wimblehurst, in Wimblehurst Road.

Park Street

An old street originally called Back Lane which linked Denne Road with North Street. Due to the redevelopment of the area in the twentieth century, Park Street has been cut in two by Park Way. A short pedestrianised stretch leading off East Street remains as Park Place and on the other side of Park Way is the short stretch leading into North Street.

The original drill hall was built here in 1873 as the headquarters of the 7th Sussex Volunteer Corps formed after the Crimean War in the 1850s. In 1908 the 4th Battalion of the Royal Sussex Regiment was formed out of the original volunteers and the regiment's crest can be seen on the front of the new drill hall opened in 1927 in Denne Road.

Park Terrace, East and West

Prior to its demolition in 1845, a gaol stood on this site. The area became known as Park Place until the railway line was extended south around 1860. This cut through the roads and the two sides became Park Place East and West, finally becoming Park Terrace East and West.

Parsonage Road and Way

The road developed from an ancient trackway across the Common. The farm here was known as Parsonage Farm because it had to pay tithes to St Mary's church which then had to pay revenue to the nuns at Rusper Priory (see Searles View). At one time the farm was owned by the Hurst family.

Until the automatic barriers were installed around 1975 the level crossing was hand-operated and closed for the night around 10 p.m. The area began to be developed between the wars when CIBA (now Novartis) first came to Horsham in 1937 and built their premises on land which had formerly belonged to the Wimblehurst Estate. In the 1960s they added a research laboratory to their premises.

Parsons Walk (1980s)

Named for Stan Parsons (see Stan's Way).

Peary Road (1970s-1980s)

This is named after Robert Peary, the Arctic explorer who reached the North Pole in his 1906-09 expedition.

Percy Road (1870s)

Another connection with the poet Percy Bysshe Shelley who lived locally (see Shelley Road and Court).

William Pirie, headmaster of Collyer's school, *c.* 1850.

Piries Place (1990)

This was still a market leading off the Carfax until the late twentieth century. In 1822 Mr Pirie was appointed by the Mercer's Co. to be headmaster of Collyer's School in Denne Road. By the 1840s he had raised the standards of teaching, attracted more pupils and new buildings had replaced the old school which had been in disrepair. He held the post of headmaster until his death in 1868. He also built a terrace of fifteen cottages just to the side of the market place, perhaps as an investment. He was very popular and just in front of Waitrose there is a sculpture of him driving his donkey and trap (see also Denne Road).

In the narrow alley or twittern linking Piries Place with the Carfax, the timber framing from medieval houses can still be seen in the walls. The houses front onto the Carfax.

Pondtail Road/Drive

Originally, this was probably a lane leading from the Warnham Road to Pondtail Farm which is some distance from Warnham millponds but there is no evidence of a closer pond. There were a few cottages close to the farm which, before the A264 was built, would have been reached by what is now Pondtail Drive. At the Warnham Road end stood at least two large old properties which now have roads named after them (see Old Millmeads and Ashleigh). There has been a Rising Sun pub since at least the early nineteenth century.

Piries Alley linking Piries Place to the Carfax. Note the medieval timbers on either side from buildings which front onto the Carfax.

Pump Alley, or Talbot Lane, about 1890.

The old post box in the wall of Pump Alley where letters would have been handed in to the postmaster.

The pentacycle invented by Edward Burstow and briefly trialled by the post office.

Park Farm was situated around halfway along Pondtail Road and Park Farm House, in Pondtail Drive, is still lived in. It is probably from this farm that Bakehouse Barn Close and Haybarn Drive take their names (see also Quarterbrass Farm Road).

Pump Alley

This is just by the Town Hall and is also known as Talbot Way having originally been Talbot Lane, another medieval alley or twittern. As the name suggests there was once a well and a pump here. The boarded-up hatch for the post office can still be seen (on the wall) through which the mail would have been handed in to the postmaster in the late nineteenth century. A Thai restaurant now stands on the site of the Talbot Inn but timbers from medieval buildings can still be seen in the walls of the alley.

Purton Road (1870s)

See Kempshott Road

Q

Quarterbrass Farm Road

This was still a farm until the late 1980s when the housing estate was built.

It is suggested that John Bolster lived here in the early twentieth century. In 1929 John and his brother Richard built a sporting cycle car known as *Bloody Mary*. With many modifications over the years, it was raced in sprints, hill climbs and circuit races before and after the Second World War and John was soon winning events. After a severe accident in the late 1940s, John gradually spent more time commentating and writing about cars than racing them. One of his books *Motoring is my business* was published in 1958. By the 1970s *Bloody Mary* was in the Beaulieu Motor Museum. There is now a John Bolster Award for Lifetime Achievement in the field of motor racing.

Queen Street

Queen Street is the continuation of East Street from just beyond the Iron Bridge and there was a brickyard near the Iron Bridge until the Second World War. The Queen's Head Inn was named for Queen Elizabeth I and the inn sign depicts her face although the road was named for Queen Victoria.

Above: Queen's Head pub sign in Queen Street, depicting Queen Elizabeth I, although the street was named for Queen Victoria.

Right: John Lawrence, the last person to be hanged in Horsham in 1844 whose body could be viewed at the Queen's Head for a small charge!

Opposite page: Queen Street in 1910.

Two previous gaols had been in the Carfax but the 'new' gaol was built in the late 1700s near the Iron Bridge extending from Park Terrace East to Park Terrace West. This gaol was large and impressive incorporating the latest designs and theories and it was the first gaol to have individual cells. John Lawrence, aged nineteen, was the last person to be hanged in public in Horsham in 1844. He had killed a police superintendent while he was being interviewed in Brighton Town Hall, by striking him over the head with a poker while the superintendent was stoking the fire. Lawrence was hanged outside the gaol in Queen Street and, for a small charge, his body could be viewed at the Queen's Head Inn. The gaol was demolished in 1845 and the railway line was built through the site.

Horsham Football Club was formed in 1870 and moved here to its present site around 1910.

R

Redkiln Way and Close (1970s)

This no doubt takes its name from the brick kilns which were here. The brickworks were closed down in the Second World War in case the furnaces could be spotted by enemy planes.

Redford Avenue (1960s)

Despite being built next to the Red River, the name is not connected as it is named after Mr Redford who built the houses. It was originally Redford Road but this tended to be confused with Bedford Road so the name was amended in 1949. Mr Redford was a president of the Trinity Cricket Club which now plays at the Victory Road recreation ground.

Red River Court built in the 1970s is named after Red River. The river is man-made and was widened and deepened to assist in taking up any flood water should the Warnham ponds overflow (the sluice gates to the pond had been breached in 1908 resulting in flooding). The 'red' refers to the fact that the iron in the water tinges it red.

Ringley Oak and Road

The big house which stood here was first called Ringley and until the 1920s was the only house in Rusper Road until reaching the post office further down towards Littlehaven Station. The reason for one owner adding 'Oak' to the name is unknown.

In the early 1900s the chief constable of the police lived here and kept the police bloodhounds. This was when the police station in Barttelot Road was the headquarters for West Sussex Police. Another owner in the 1960s was Brigadier Whitworth who was the first district commissioner of Crawley Scouts.

The house was demolished and the flats built in 1965. Ringley Road is built in what was once the orchard of the big house.

Rookwood Park (1990s)

This was once Rookwood Farm.

Rough Way (1960s)

This name reflects that Roffey was originally 'Rough Hey' meaning deer park.

Rushams Road

There were fields and a barn known as Rusham's barn dating back perhaps to the seventeenth century. There is a suggestion that possibly the North Parade end of the road might have been a carriageway to Springfield Park. Housing at this end was built in the late nineteenth century and, more or less opposite Holy Trinity church, one of the cottages was a doll's hospital. These cottages were demolished and a petrol station built but now the site has reverted to housing. The road did not extend to the Guildford Road until after the Second World War so the housing here is mid-twentieth century.

Lilian Franklin lived in Rushams Road until her death in 1955 at the age of ninety-four. She was commanding officer of, and also responsible for restructuring, FANY. These initials stand for First Aid Nursing Yeomanry, an organisation set up in 1907. During the First and Second World Wars its members served as a link between the front line and the field hospitals. It has now been renamed the Princess Royal Volunteer Corps, FANY (PRVC) and is always on call and has seen service in Iraq.

The land on which Holy Trinity church was built around 1900 was known as Birds Farm. This had once been owned by Elizabeth Gatford in the late 1700s (see North Street).

Ryders Way (1980 and 1990s)

This is named for Ryders Farm. The farmhouse, in Northlands Road, is still lived in today. The farm was in existence perhaps from as early as the thirteenth century.

S

Sandeman Way (late 1930s)

This road and Hernbrook Drive are built on the site of Hernbrook House. This had been built in 1830 by William Sandeman, grandson of the founder of the well-known port wine firm, when he married Mary, younger daughter of George Bax Holmes (see Causeway).

The house was demolished in around the 1920s but the coach house has been restored and is now a retirement home. The core of the coach house is much older and, on the opposite side of what was the carriageway to the big house, is another very old property dated to 1658. During the nineteenth century it was the gardener's cottage and the tenant paid rent of 1d for the house and 1d for the well in the garden. Most of the original structure still exists and the house has been beautifully and sympathetically restored.

Saxon Way (1950s)

A reminder that Horsham was once a Saxon settlement

Searles View (1980 and 1990s)

The Searles family have lived at Parsonage Farm for many years (it is no longer farmed) and when the new road was built it was called Searles View as the residents looked out onto the land owned by the Searles family. The first son has always been named Les and the present Les runs the agricultural contracting business. His brother James owns a large collection of steam vehicles which always featured prominently in the town carnivals and hospital fêtes, particularly the steam organ. Both businesses were built up by their father after the Second World War (see Parsonage Road).

Shelley Road and Court (before 1900)

These are named for the Shelleys who were a prominent family in and around Horsham from the sixteenth century. The famous poet Percy Bysshe Shelley was born in 1792 at Field Place, Broadbridge Heath. It would seem that he spent a very happy early childhood there with his sisters and his cousins. He used to enjoy playing with them and friends at Warnham ponds.

He received his first schooling in Warnham before going to Sion Academy near London. Thereafter he went on to Eton and Oxford University. He had started writing poetry at an early age and by 1810 was publishing verse and novels. He was expelled from Oxford in 1811 for having written *The Necessity of Atheism* which was publicly denounced. He was becoming a passionate idealist and his writings railed against politics, social inequalities and religion, and were definitely anti-establishment. He fell out with his father, Sir Timothy (MP for Horsham 1790-92) and having been expelled from Oxford rarely ever went back to Field Place. He got on slightly better with his grandfather, Sir Bysshe Shelley, who lived at Arun House in Denne Road for some twenty years and who helped him financially.

In August 1811 he eloped with and married Harriet Westbrook and they lived in Ireland and Devon. His poem *Queen Mab* was published at this time. By July 1814 he had fallen in love with Mary Wollstonecraft and eloped with her. They lived both in London and on the continent but were shunned by nearly everyone. In 1816 Harriet drowned and he promptly married Mary and, due to poor health and financial difficulties, they went to live in Italy in 1818. He and Mary had four children but only Percy Florence Shelley, born in 1819, survived infancy. Mary is perhaps best remembered as the author of *Frankenstein* which she begun in 1816. Percy Bysshe Shelly drowned in 1822 when his yacht capsized in the Gulf of Spezia, Italy.

The poet's son, Percy Florence Shelley, inherited Field Place when his grandfather Sir Timothy died in 1844. He rose to high office and became Deputy Lord Lieutenant and High Sheriff of Sussex.

The sculpture of Rising Universe, more often referred to as the Shelley Fountain, discharging its water, which was erected in West Street in the 1990s.

The poet continued wrote prolifically but not all of his work was published during his lifetime as it was neither popular nor appreciated either then or for a long while thereafter and it was not until the late twentieth century that his works began to be properly understood and valued and a sculpture, officially called Rising Universe, but often referred to as the Shelley Monument or Fountain commemorating the poet was erected in West Street in the 1990s.

Shelley Road is close to the site of Spencers Farm which at one time was owned by his father, Sir Timothy Shelley. Shelley Court is in North Horsham.

The poet also had a famous uncle – John Pilfold. Pilfold's sister had married Timothy Shelley. Pilfold had been born and baptised in Horsham in 1769 although the family connections were with Warnham, Effingham and Cuckfield. Pilfold had entered the Navy at an early age and in 1805 was appointed acting captain of the battleship *Ajax* which fought alongside the *Victory* at the Battle of Trafalgar. He saw distinguished service and was one of the first people to be made a Commander of the Bath. This was a new military honour instituted at the end of the Napoleonic Wars in 1815. Pilfold died in 1834.

Shepherds Way (1970s)

Arthur Adolphus Shepherd was a county and district councillor in the 1960s. He ran a newsagent's shop by the station (where Shaw's Glass is now).

Smithbarn

Smiths Barn Farm provides this name and at one time this part of Comptons Lane was called Smiths Barn Lane. The Forest Community School has now been built over the farm.

South Grove (1970 and 1980s)

This was the property to which Sir Cecil Hurst moved in 1958 (prior to this he had lived in the Nunnery at Rusper which had been in the Hurst family since the sixteenth century). He was a president of the Permanent Court of International Justice at The Hague. He also held office in numerous local concerns.

Where South Grove runs into Kennedy Road there used to be a roller skating rink, just opposite East Parade School. Legend has it that the organ which provided the music for the skating rink was buried under the forecourt of the Wilson Purves garage which fronted onto the Brighton Road. East Gate Mews has now been built there.

South Holmes Road (1970-1980s)

Named after the farm which stood here. The farmer's name was Mr Gillett; hence also Gillett Court.

Both Lintotts and then Evershed & Cripps had their grocery/provisions shop in this building on the corner of South Street and Middle Street. The hoist used for raising supplies to the warehouse above the shop is still there today although the building is now occupied by the Abbey National.

South Street

One of the original roads leading off the Carfax towards St Mary's church. It was not until the sixteenth century that the name 'Causeway' was used for the stretch from the church to the Town Hall and thus South Street is now only a very short road.

A branch of the Lintott family had their retail grocers/provisions shop on the corner with Middle Street and the hoist which was used to raise supplies to the warehouse above can still be seen on what is now the Abbey National building (see Lintott Gardens). This shop will perhaps be better known as Evershed & Cripps who were also grocers and occupied the premises in the mid-twentieth century.

Spencers Place and Road

Housing estates built in the 1950s covered land which had been Spencers Farm. The lane to the farmhouse can still be seen today, close to Collingwood Road, but the farmhouse is no longer there. In the eighteenth century the farm was owned by Sir Timothy Shelley, father of the poet, Percy Bysshe Shelley.

Springfield Road in the early 1900s.

Springfield Park House which was built in the late 1700s.

The new 'Y' centre built in 2004 which stands on the corner of Springfield Road and Albion Way. It belongs to the YMCA but provides housing for both men and women.

Springfield Road, Park and Crescent

This leads from West Street to North Parade as part of the old route to London. It is so called because there were natural springs in the ground.

In the 1650s, Elias Blunt bought the property called Dyers which had been here since the 1300s. This was demolished and Springfield Park House was built by his grandson Samuel in 1758. The Blunts lived here until 1800 and then let the house to various people. The house was converted to a school in 1887. By 1890 the property housed Horsham College and remained a boys' school until 1955 and was then a girls' school until 1988. The house has now been converted into apartments and Blunt's Way and Cedar Close were built over part of the grounds.

In the early 1800s this road was also known as Chapel Lane. A chapel had been built on a piece of land which had formed part of Swan Meadow (behind the Swan Inn in West Street) in 1814 (see Morth Gardens). This was replaced later that century with the Congregational church. In the late twentieth century, the Congregational church was replaced by the present United Reformed church. The graveyard to the Congregational church has now been built over with an office block and the multi-storey car park.

In 1865, the Duchess of Norfolk built a Roman Catholic chapel here. In the early twentieth century this was replaced with the present St John's church.

There was a malt house not far from the London Road owned by the Allen family. It was raided in 1857 by the excise officers who found a large quantity of malt on which duty had not been paid. It had been hidden behind false walls and possibly down a secret tunnel which led to fields opposite. This tunnel was discovered when Albion Way was constructed in the late twentieth century. The name of the pub, the Malt Shovel, is a reminder of both the brewery and the malt house.

The Gas & Coke Co. was formed in 1835 and the gasworks originally stood opposite the Malt Shovel pub (where the new 'Y' centre has just been built) before being moved to the Redkiln Industrial Estate.

The British School was built near London Road in around 1827.

Development of Springfield Park and Springfield Crescent began in around the 1920s and was continued after the Second World War.

Stan's Way (1990s)

Named after Stan Parsons who was born in 1905 in Albion Terrace (demolished when Albion Way was constructed). His grandparents ran the Crown Hotel in the Carfax and at one time Stan lived there. As a young man he served in the Merchant Navy as a radio operator. He then took over a newsagent's shop in the Carfax which he and his wife ran for some forty years. He was in the Royal Observer Corps before and during the first part of the Second World War before joining the RAF. During the Second World War, Stan was the driving force in raising funds which enabled the town to present a Spitfire aeroplane to the MOD and, together with Crawley village, a submarine.

After the war Stan became ever more involved in Horsham affairs. He served on the council for thirty-eight years, holding office as chairman for three terms. Among many other interests he was involved with the chamber of trade, was a founder member of the Horsham Society and a president of The Museum Society.

For many years he lived in Springfield Park Road and died at the age of ninety-three. He was known affectionately as 'Mr Horsham' and worked tirelessly all his life in helping the town (see Athelstan Way, Parsons Walk and Hengist Close).

Standen Place (1990s)

See Uppark Gardens.

Stan's Way, named for Stan Parsons, which leads off Piries Place.

Stanley Street Steam Laundry, *c.* 1900.

Stanley Walk

Originally this was Stanley Street and the Electric Lighting Works were opened here in 1902. All the town's refuse was brought here to be sorted and then the appropriate refuse was burnt in the furnace which provided the power for the generators. When additional roads were built the only remaining part of the street was renamed Stanley Walk (see Livingstone Road and Victoria Street).

St Leonard's Road

This road leads to the forest. It originally stopped where you can now turn on to Hammerpond Road. This forest is part of the ancient forest which covered a large area of this part of the country.

Iron working in the forest was a very important industry for centuries. The Romans used the forest as a rich source of iron and the industry flourished again from the thirteenth to the sixteenth centuries. Five rivers rise in the forest, the Arun being the one which runs through Horsham. Water was therefore plentiful – necessary for the hammer ponds – together with the timber for charcoal. The forest was dotted with dwellings ranging from substantial homes

Mick Miles' Race in St Leonard's forest, around 1894 or earlier.

for the iron masters to the huts used by the charcoal burners. Close to Dickins Way there is a very old barn roofed with Horsham stone. By the hammer pond is a very old house which might have been lived in by an iron master.

There were also farms in the clearings and possibly a chapel from the thirteenth century. Mention is made in the sixteenth century of a chapel dedicated to St Leonard.

There was a large estate known as St Leonard's Park (near to Hampers Lane) which was lived in during the twentieth century by the Latilla family. Coolhurst was the property of the Dickins family. There was also Forest Grange School.

Many myths and legends have evolved over the centuries, especially that of the dragon. St Leonard was a 'popular' saint in early times and he is supposed to have slain the dragon who lived here. He was a very long-lived dragon as he was 'seen' as late as the seventeenth century!

The forest was ideal for smugglers bringing their goods up from the south coast on their way to London. One of the ponds is known as Hawkins Pond after a smuggling gang and a Squire Paullet is said to haunt travellers as a headless ghost on horseback.

Another legend is that of Mick Miles. He was a smuggler who used the forest and on one occasion it is said that the Devil came to him wanting his soul. Mick challenged the Devil to a race down a mile-long avenue of fir trees. Mick won and the Devil never hounded him again. Race Hill and Mick's Cross are still shown on maps (see also Hammerpond Road, Forest Road, Leechpool Lane, Coolhurst Lane and Copperfields).

Swan Walk (1980s)

This shopping mall off West Street is built where the old coaching inn The Swan fronted on to West Street. The inn sign is now in Horsham Museum. Part of the area behind the pub was known as Swan Meadow – now the multi-storey car park (see West Street).

Swindon Road (1880s)

See Kempshott Road.

The entrance to Swan Walk, from West Street.

T

Talbot Lane

See Pump Alley

Tanbridge Park and Place (late 1990s)

There was a tannery here from the 1400s from which the bridge took its name. Just over the bridge in Worthing Road and dating back to the 1400s was a property known as Cadmans, subsequently Nyes. One owner was Mrs Killick, the last person to be buried at night in 1829; this had been fashionable then, with a torchlight procession from the church! A new property, Tanbridge House, was built by Thomas Oliver in 1887 (see Oliver Road). The house, with its ornate chimneys, is now apartments and is in the middle of the new Tanbridge Park housing estate. From 1924 to 1975 the house was used as the Girls' High School. In 1975 this became Tanbridge House School and was a co-ed comprehensive school. In 1994 the school moved to Farthings Hill on the Guildford Road.

Tanbridge House, built by Thomas Oliver in 1887. The house is now apartments in the middle of Tanbridge Park Estate.

Tanyard Close (1970s)

This is named for the old tannery which used to stand where Queen Street becomes Brighton Road. The cast-iron pillars came from London and are still to be seen at the Chalkpits Museum at Amberley. The blacksmiths connected with the tannery had a 'spreading chestnut tree' beside it – for a very good reason. Apparently, flies will not gather under a chestnut tree so the horses were not tormented by them whilst being shod.

Thatchers Close (1980s)

Like Heath Way this is named for a British Prime Minister.

Tower Hill and Close

The tower for which there is documented evidence was more a folly than a tower as it stood only 18ft high. It was built in the late nineteenth century and was demolished in the 1920s when one of the houses in this ancient hamlet was bought by a master from Christ's Hospital. He had the tower pulled down as it obstructed his view of Horsham. It would seem from old maps that there was a 'proper' tower in earlier times but nothing is known about it.

Trafalgar Road (1870-80s)

Trafalgar, Victory and Nelson Roads (not forgetting the Nelson Pub) were built at the edge of the Common in around the 1870s. They were named to commemorate (rather tardily!) the Battle of Trafalgar which had taken place in 1805.

This area was known as the 'back of the Common' and then 'the Common' and right up until the middle of the twentieth century was a close knit community with many small, local shops. The only remaining part of the Common is the grassed area by the Dog & Bacon pub.

Victory Road School (where Trafalgar School is now) was badly burned in 1940 and the children were temporarily moved to other schools; some to British Legion huts in North Street.

Treadcroft Drive (1980s)

This was named after the Revd Nathaniel Tredcroft who at one time owned the Manor House and should not have the 'a' in its name (see Causeway).

U

Uppark Gardens (1990s)

This road, together with Standen Place, Cissbury Close, Petworth Drive, Highdown Way, Nymans Close and Bignor Close are all named after local National Trust properties.

Vernon Close (1970s)

Col. Vernon was for many years a church warden at St Mary's church in the mid-twentieth century. He was a First World War veteran and was very much a 'man of the parish'. He lived in Ashleigh Road.

Victoria Street

Named for Queen Victoria when the waterworks were built here in around 1865. However, as the townspeople were most reluctant to spend money on drainage and sewerage, it was not until the 1880s, when forced by the Government, that things began to improve. It was when this road and Livingstone Road were built that Stanley Street became truncated.

Victory Road (1870s)

See Trafalgar Road

Vincent Close (1980 and 1990s)

Gerald Vincent was in the choir of St Mary's church and a chairman of Horsham Urban District Council. Gerald Court is also named after him.

W

Wallis Way (1980s)

This is named for Sir Barnes Wallis, the aeronautical designer who is well remembered for his bouncing bomb used in the Dam Busters Raid during the Second World War.

He was born in 1887 and attended Christ's Hospital School from 1900-1904 and kept his connection with the school when he became treasurer to the almoners, helped redesign some of the buildings and helped raise over £1million for the school. He died in 1979.

Warnham Road

This is the continuation of North Parade on the route to Dorking and London. One suggestion for the name of the Dog & Bacon pub is that it was first called The Dorking Beacon (try saying Dorking Beacon quickly!). There has been a pub here since at least the late 1700s; however, in earlier times it was housed in the old cottages which stand to one side of the present pub built around 1900.

The Dog & Bacon pub around 1900. Prior to 1900 the pub was housed next door in the old cottages. The only remaining part of the Common is the grassed area by the pub.

Warnham Mill in Warnham Road. There has been a mill here since the 1300s and this building dates back to the seventeenth century.

The Vanderbilt coach which ran between London and Brighton, calling at the Dog & Bacon and the Crown Hotel in the Carfax, pictured in 1912.

In the first years of the twentieth century, a Mr A.G. Vanderbilt (not the American millionaire) was so taken with the Sussex and Surrey countryside that he ran coaches from London to Brighton passing through Horsham. The coaches used to stop at both the Dog & Bacon and the Crown Inn in the Carfax.

Shortly past the Dog & Bacon is Warnham Mill. This has been the site of a mill since the 1300s and the present building dates back to the seventeenth century and is the oldest surviving mill in Horsham. Originally the two ponds powered an iron furnace but it was later used as a flour mill until the twentieth century.

The property was once owned by the Shelley family and Percy Bysshe Shelley spent happy hours playing here as a child. It was also very popular when it froze in the winter as folk went there to skate. In 1870 the miller was William Prewett who owned Prewett's Mill in the Worthing Road.

In 1906 the sluice gates breached, a large area was flooded and hundreds of fish were stranded and died. More recently the old mill building has been used as offices with Warnham Nature Reserve centred around the ponds.

Wellington Road

This road was built in the late nineteenth century and named after Sir Arthur Wellesley who was created Duke of Wellington in 1814 following the Battle of Waterloo in 1812. In addition to his outstanding military achievements he also spent many years in parliament and was Prime Minister from 1828-30. He was appointed Lord High Constable of England in 1848 and died in 1852 at the age of eighty-three (see Corunna Drive).

West Parade

This used to be known as Figgs Lane after a Mr Figg who lived just opposite at Greenacres in North Parade. During the Second World War Greenacres was an hotel and subsequently a home for maladjusted children. It has now been demolished and flats built on the site.

Before the Second World War there were only houses on one side of West Parade with more being built at the same time as Newlands Road was extended to West Parade. There used to be a large house where the Smith & Weston restaurant now stands which gave its name to the present houses in the Walnuts. Tulip Court on the opposite corner is named after the large tulip tree *Liriodendron tulipifera* which once grew there and is possibly sprouting again.

Above: West Street in 1906.

Right: Clerkenwell House in West Street. It was originally Jury Cramp's premises in the 1870s and still a jewellers today.

West Street

One of the original streets leading off the Carfax. A poultry market was held here from the 1400s and then a corn market. It was and still is a busy shopping area. The Swan Inn stood just at the entrance to Swan Walk.

West Street ends by the sculptured fountain in memory of Percy Bysshe Shelley, officially called Rising Universe, just by the Lynd Cross Pub and McDonald's.

William Albery, mentioned under Albery Close, was born in 1864 above the saddlery shop at No. 49 West Street and took over his father's saddlery and harness-making business. In addition to helping establish Horsham Museum to which he donated many items, he was also a noted historian and author of three important books about Horsham: *The Parliamentary History of Horsham, A Millennium of facts in the History of Horsham and Sussex* and Henry Burstow's *Reminiscences of Horsham* (see Albery Close).

Mr Jury Cramp came to Horsham in the 1870s and established his jeweller's shop in West Street. He named the premises Clerkenwell House as he had served his apprenticeship in Clerkenwell, London and the name can still be seen above the shop. His family traded there for 100 years and the premises are still a jeweller's shop today. He was a well-known figure in Horsham, a staunch member of the Methodist church and was a lifelong member of the Temperance Society (see Market Square).

His grandson, Cecil, was still running the shop in the late twentieth century but is remembered even more for his extensive collection of images and photos which provide such an excellent record of the town. He also gave many talks on Horsham.

The Horsham Hoard, found in West Street, is mentioned under Honeywood Road.

White Hart Court (1960s)

This was once the site of the White Hart pub in North Parade.

Wildgoose Drive (late 1990s)

Until the late nineteenth century, both Great and Little Wildgoose Farms occupied this land but Wildgoose Drive was not built until the late twentieth century.

Wimblehurst Road

A little way before the road now bears left into North Heath Lane stood a post windmill. Over time the name was corrupted firstly to Windmill Post Farm, then to Wimbel Post and finally settled into Wimblehurst – why Post changed to Hurst is not clear!

Wimblehurst Lodge is still there but the large Victorian house has been demolished. It was in the area of land between North Heath Lane and Parsonage Road. Owners

Picts Hill as this stretch of the Worthing Road was known, in 1904, showing the Boar's Head pub, previously called the Fox & Hounds.

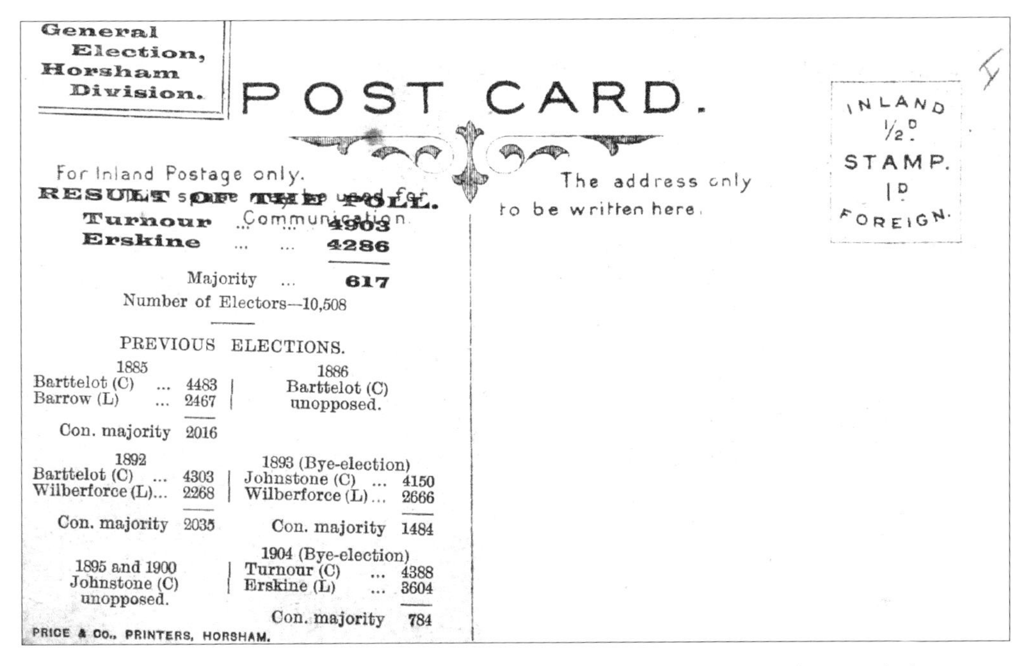

General Election, Horsham Division.

POST CARD.

For Inland Postage only. This space may be used for Communication.

The address only to be written here.

INLAND ½D STAMP. 1D FOREIGN.

RESULT OF THE POLL.

Turnour	...	4903
Erskine	... ...	4286
Majority	...	617

Number of Electors—10,508

PREVIOUS ELECTIONS.

1885

Barttelot (C)	...	4483
Barrow (L)	...	2467
Con. majority		2016

1886

Barttelot (C) unopposed.

1892

Barttelot (C)	...	4303
Wilberforce (L)...		2268
Con. majority		2035

1893 (Bye-election)

Johnstone (C)	...	4150
Wilberforce (L) ...		2666
Con. majority		1484

1895 and 1900

Johnstone (C) unopposed.

1904 (Bye-election)

Turnour (C)	...	4388
Erskine (L)	...	3604
Con. majority		784

PRICE & CO., PRINTERS, HORSHAM.

Reverse side of the postcard on the next page announcing the results of the 1906 election which was won by Edward Turnour, later Earl Winterton.

Front side of the same postcard showing the Town Hall during the 1906 election.

included Henry Padwick Jnr (see Padwick Road) and the Allcard family who were great benefactors of Horsham, supporting various worthwhile causes (see Allcard Close).

Windrum Close (1980s)

Anthony Windrum was a councillor in the mid-twentieth century and is also well known as an author of books on local history including *Horsham – an Historical Survey*.

Winterton Court (1970s)

Edward Turnour, born 1883, became the sixth Earl Winterton. He was elected as MP at the age of twenty-one in 1904 and held office continuously until 1951 when he was created Baron Turnour. He first represented Horsham and Worthing and then just Horsham when the constituencies were divided. He died in 1962 (see Market Square).

Lynde Cottage in Worthing Road, dating back to the 1400s.

The new bus station in Worthing Road, built in 2003.

Mill Bay, near Provender and Prewett's Mills, close to the entrance to Sainsbury's, taken before 1926.

Provender Mill which was the town mill, now offices.

Prewett's Mill, now offices.

Christ's Hospital School in 1907, which had been opened by the Prince of Wales (later King Edward VI) in 1902.

Worthing Road

Travellers were crossing the River Arun over the tan bridge from at least the fifteenth century. The bridge was so called because of the tannery close by. Originally the route to the south coast went through Denne Park but by the mid-1700s, Worthing Road had been turnpiked and travellers left town over the tan bridge. There was a toll gate by the bridge and another one further on near the Boar's Head pub. Because horses found it very hard going up the steep Picts Hill, the road was lowered to make it easier for them.

Before going out of town over the bridge, there is the Friends Meeting House (Quakers), built in 1786. Ambrose Rigge, a well known Quaker, was imprisoned in Horsham Gaol in 1662 for ten years. George Fox, another well known Quaker, preached in Horsham in 1655. The Unitarian church is next to Lynde Cottage. The cottage dates back to the 1400s and the junction of Springfield Road and West Street (where McDonald's is now) was known as the Lynd Cross which is why the name has been revived for the pub. Just opposite the cottage but some five centuries later, the new bus station was opened in 2003.

There were two mills in the Worthing Road. Provender Mill was the town mill and had belonged to Rusper Nunnery from as early as the thirteenth century. It can be reached down Mill Bay Lane. Prewett's Mill faces onto the Worthing Road just by the entrance to Sainsbury's (the name is still on the front of the building). From the 1860s it was owned by William Prewett (who, in 1870, was the miller at Warnham Mill) and the mill was still producing flour well into the twentieth century. Both of the mills can still be seen today and have been converted into offices. Mill Bay which was close to both mills was a favourite place for swimming right into the twentieth century.

Turning right by the Boar's Head pub (formerly the Fox & Hounds) leads to Christ's Hospital School which was moved here from London and was opened by the Prince of Wales in 1902. This area used to be a quarry for Horsham stone and was known as Stammerham. This is a Saxon word meaning 'dwelling by stone pit'. The Michell family owned a large property here in the nineteenth century and they had interests in many local businesses such as brewing, brickworks, the railway and the waterworks (see Michell Close).

XYZ

York Close (1980s)

The name of the Close and the four blocks of flats in the Close bear Royal Dynasty names – Windsor Court, Tudor House, Hanover Court and Stuart House.

Index of Street Names

Other local titles published by Tempus

Haunted Guildford

PHILIP HUTCHINSON

Haunted Guildford contains a chilling range of ghostly accounts. From tales of a piano-playing spirit at Guildford Museum and a spectral monk who wanders up Friary Street, to stories of a poltergeist at the Three Pigeons public house and sightings of a ghostly woman on Whitmoor Common, this selection is sure to appeal to anyone interested in the supernatural history of the area.

0 7524 3826 3

Horsham

SUSAN DJABRI

This collection of nearly 200 images, mostly drawn from the collections of Horsham Museum, and many never before published, provides a fascinating pictorial history of Horsham over the last two centuries. Horsham is a valuable pictorial record of the town's history, which will awaken nostalgic memories for some, while offering a unique glimpse of the past for others.

0 7524 3831 X

Basingstoke

MALCOLM PARKER

Basingstoke has been established for over 1,000 years and yet it is often seen by outsiders as a new town, a town which was barely on the map before its major redevelopment in the 1960s. This book focuses on the gradual development over the past two centuries with over 200 photographs, maps and images illustrating people and places that have featured and shaped its colourful history.

7978 07524 3082 9

Bognor Regis

SYLVIA ENDACOTT AND SHIRLEY LEWIS

Bognor Regis today is a vibrant seaside resort. As well as boasting one of the oldest piers in Britain the town is known for Billy Butlin and his impact on bringing bucket-loads of holiday makers to the resort. Visitors and residents old and new will enjoy seeing the faces of the people and the buildings over the centuries that have made Bognor Regis what it is today.

978 07524 42990

If you are interested in purchasing other books published by Tempus, or in case you have difficulty finding any Tempus books in your local bookshop, you can also place orders directly through our website

www.tempus-publishing.com